Win the Astro[...] with Tri-Astral Analysis

What are the astrology games people play? Modern psychology believes that your public personality is the result of an interior drama—or game—played out by your own inner "actors." The way you express yourself is the result of a tug-of-war by your inner actors, whose game-playing or ways of interacting fall into patterns which can be modified to achieve growth and personal goals.

Astrology Games People Play will teach you a how to use a unique and effective method for identifying these patterns: Tri-Astral analysis. The key to the success of this analytical tool is its combination of the three-ring graphics, representing the ego states, and the esoteric and symbolic depths of astrology. Tri-Astral analysis makes it easier than ever before for anyone to marry astrological information with basic modern psychology to gain insights about themselves and their loved ones.

In which area of your life do you have the greatest number of conflicting issues? If these conflicts are causing you pain, it could mean that one area of your personality is—in astro-analysis terms—overly "weighted." Using the information from your birth chart, you can quickly construct your own Tri-Astral chart and get a strikingly clear, graphic representation of the different positive and negative polarities within your personality—allowing you to discover and start working on emotionally difficult areas and clear away the emotional debris of the past.

Determine the attitudes of the key mental players in your own inner "games" of love and life for self-healing, to help you evaluate your relationships, and to open new doors to understanding the games you and others play!

"**This is an excellent book for all astrologers** who wish to guide their clients into using this wonderful road map we call the horoscope in an intelligent, yet easy, way."

— Marion D. March
Aspects magazine

"Through its straightforwardness and Spencer Grendahl's genuine eagerness to elucidate the facts very carefully, **this book becomes an extremely useful guide.** It might very well become a best-seller!"

— Stephanie Forest
Considerations magazine

"**Spencer Grendahl knows how to get to the core of people.** He is more than an astrologer. He brings psychological insights to his readers on every page."

— Fred Amsel
Theatrical agent

"Spencer Grendahl has a good heart. **You can feel his sincerity in his book.** He taught me a lot about astrology and people."

— Angela Visser
Miss Universe 1989

"Spencer Grendahl has a delightful way of pegging exactly who you are. **The new process that he's developed is fascinating,** fun to do, and more importantly, a truly valuable insight into who we are and why we do the crazy things we do."

— Margrit Polak
Personal manager and acting coach

About the Author

Spencer Grendahl has been involved in metaphysical studies since 1965, when a friend's grandmother pronounced him a psychic and a maverick. While Spencer did complete degrees at Brown and Harvard, and for a while was a teacher and curriculum developer, his true interest in writing and metaphysics led him to Los Angeles where he studied astrology with Marion March and other prominent astrologers.

Spencer's natural intuitive skills and outgoing personality soon enabled him to become a professional metaphysical reader. He has done readings for a variety of Hollywood stars as well as social and political figures in Los Angeles. He has lectured in the United States, the United Kingdom, and Australia.

Spencer is the author of a novel (*Mad Dog*) and a movie (*Street Soldiers*), as well as new age books: *The Secrets of Love, Romance on Your Hands*, and *Astrology and the Games People Play*. He is an avid scuba diver, flute player, and public speaker.

To Write to the Author

If you wish to contact the author or would like more information about this book, please write to the author in care of Llewellyn Worldwide, and we will forward your request. Both the author and the publisher appreciate hearing from you and learning of your enjoyment of this book and how it has helped you. Llewellyn Worldwide cannot guarantee that every letter written to the author can be answered, but all will be forwarded. Please write to:

Spencer Grendahl
c/o Llewellyn Worldwide
P.O. Box 64383-338, St. Paul, MN 55164-0383, U.S.A.

Please enclose a self-addressed, stamped envelope or $1.00 to cover costs.
If outside the U.S.A., enclose international postal reply coupon.

Free Catalog from Llewellyn

For more than 90 years Llewellyn has brought its readers knowledge in the fields of metaphysics and human potential. Learn about the newest books in spiritual guidance, natural healing, astrology, occult philosophy and more. Enjoy book reviews, new age articles, a calendar of events, plus current advertised products and services. To get your free copy of *Llewellyn's New Worlds of Mind and Spirit*, send your name and address to:

Llewellyn's New Worlds of Mind and Spirit
P.O. Box 64383-338, St. Paul, MN 55164-0383, U.S.A.

Astrology and the Games People Play

A Tool for Self-Understanding in Work
and Relationships

Spencer Grendahl

1994
Llewellyn Publications
St. Paul, Minnesota, 55164-0383, U.S.A.

FIRST EDITION
First Printing, 1994

Cover Art: Ken Shibata
Cover Design: Linda Norton
Book Design and Layout: Susan Van Sant
Editing: Susan Van Sant and Jessica Thoreson

Library of Congress Cataloging-in-Publication Data
Grendahl, Spencer.
    Astrology and the games people play: a tool for self-understanding in work and relationships / Spencer Grendahl.
      p.   cm.
    ISBN 1-56718-338-7
    1. Astrology and psychology. 2. Inner child—Miscellanea. 3. Self-perception—Miscellanea. 4. Interpersonal relations—Miscellanea. I. Title.
    BF1729.P8G77 1994
    133.5—dc20   93-48354
                                                CIP

Llewellyn Publications
A Division of Llewellyn Worldwide, Ltd.
P.O. Box 64383, St. Paul, MN 55164-0383

Printed in the United States of America

★ ★ ☆ ★ ★ ☆ ★ ☆

Dedication

To my wife Katie,
who inspired and endured
the writing of this book.

★ ★ ☆ ★ ★ ☆ ★ ☆

Acknowledgments

First, without Joan McEvers publishing my first effort in Tri-Astral analysis as a chapter in *The Web of Relationships*, this book might not have been written. Without Marion March as my teacher during my formative years, I would not have had the astrological drive to take new ideas seriously. I want to thank Los Angeles's NCGR Chapter for listening to and critiquing the early versions of this concept. Arthyr Chadbourne gave me the benefit of his many years as an astrologer. Leigh Tobias, who is both an astrologer and a practicing psychologist, read and commented on all of the drafts. To Leigh I owe a special debt for all the details she pointed out. Finally, to Paul Ingram, the graphic designer, for all the new and different charts, especially the family circle.

★ ★ ☆ ★ ★ ☆ ★ ☆

Table of Contents

★ ★ ☆ ☆ ☆ ☆ ★ ★

Figure 1

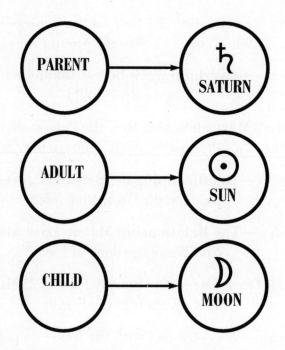

**Translating popular ego states
psychology into a Tri-Astral chart**

There is a rainbow bridge
where healing knowledge
finds golden understanding.
It starts as fire in the heavens
and ends smoldering in you —
a child of a starburst.

★ ★ ☆ ★ ☆ ★ ★ ☆

Introduction

Discovering Tri-Astral Astrology

did it!" Angelica's voice rang clear on the phone. "I told Rick to take a hike if he wasn't going to treat me right. I feel so good, Spencer. My Inner Moon/Child thanks you. I'm going to find a man who can love me." Angelica had been working through a personal Tri-Astral astrology program for three months. She started out knowing little of either psychology or astrology.

At first glance, astrology looks easy. You construct a chart which shows the positions of the Sun, Moon, and planets at the time of a person's birth. From these fundamental points of planetary energy, one can build a mosaic reflecting a kaleidoscope of insight. However, this ancient craft can become more and more complex. There is a specialized vocabulary including words like grand trines, T-squares, yods, learning triangles, grand crosses, transits, and progressions, to name a few. In-depth astrology requires long and serious study.

As an astrologer, I have been constantly aware of the difficulty of communicating simple astrological concepts. Explaining the "ABCs" of the natal

———— ★ xi ★ ————

chart to beginners is tricky work. Even the fundamentals are sometimes hard to get across and may require the use of extensive teaching skills.

Tri-Astral astrology, the subject of this book, was created while trying to teach some rudimentary astrological insights to a client who was struggling to understand her natal chart. Angelica was a sincere young woman who had come for a personal consultation. She knew nothing of astrology and could not seem to grasp what I was trying to communicate. It was Greek to her. What could I do?

My stress level was rising, for I pride myself on being clear and patient. With Angelica looking at me with the glassy eyes of incomprehension, I feverishly racked my brain. I wanted her to get an understanding about what astrology was saying about her Inner Child. She needed to see that an inner fear was holding her back; something she'd experienced while very young had established a repetitive and restrictive pattern, undermining her adulthood.

On a hunch I asked her, "Do you know how some psychologists depict the personality by using three rings to represent the Parent, Adult, and Child in our minds?" Angelica nodded yes; a small glimmer of comprehension was starting. We had found something to use as a reference. "Well," I continued, taking a sheet of paper and drawing three circles (figure 1), "What if we said your Moon was a symbol of your Inner Child, the Sun was your Adult, and Saturn was your Parent?"

Angelica looked at the rings with great interest. She was starting to "get" my presentation of the astrological materials. Seizing the moment, I went on. "When we add the other planets that aspect or relate to your Moon, look what happens to your Moon or Inner Child. See how it is 'overloaded,' trying to do too much." With a knowing flourish I finished this quick diagram, which she studied (figure 2). Suddenly Angelica was very animated. She got my point! The key was the Inner Child.

Angelica understood the three-ring model used in popular psychology to depict three basic ego states—the Parent, Adult, and Child. She recalled that she had read an article in a women's magazine which used the three-tier graphic. This formed a bridge by which Angelica went on to understand my point about how her Inner Child had been restricted. She worked on the issues of nurturing her Inner Child. This insight helped her to make great steps toward taking control of her life. She was more successful at her work and stopped dating abusive men.

After discovering this method of Tri-Astral astrology with Angelica, I started testing my three-ring innovation on other clients unfamilar with

Figure 2

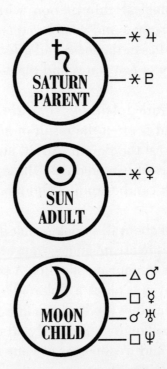

Angelica's Tri-Astral chart:
note emphasis on Moon/Child
A table of symbols is in Appendix D.
A table of aspects is in Appendix C.
Consult them to define her analysis.

astrology. They, too, responded to astrology presented in a framework that they could easily visualize. However, I was suspicious of my success for I distrusted the "purity" of the three-circle approach. The big circle of the Zodiac—that was the "real astrology." Nevertheless, when I was stuck for ways to communicate astrology to beginning clients, out would come the three circles of the Tri-Astral approach. Inevitably a reciprocal chord would be struck, and the client would start responding to the themes of my consultation.

This book will teach you to use the proven skills of Tri-Astral astrology to expand your self-awareness and personal growth. It will enable you to combine simple astrological information with modern psychology and gain insights about yourselves and your loved ones. The key to the success of this method, of course, lies in the loose and affectionate marriage of the three-ring model of the theory of ego states and the esoteric and symbolic depths of the Zodiac.

This book is entitled *Astrology and the Games People Play* because our public temperament is often the result of an inner drama or game played by three major personas: the Parent, Adult, and Child. Personal expression is a tug-of-war of inner subpersonalities whose interaction or game playing falls into patterns which can be studied and modified to achieve growth and personal goals.

What is unusual about this book is that it uses simple astrological and psychological principles to create an accurate and meaningful symbolic picture of the energy patterns in your personality. A picture, it is said, is worth a thousand words. If someone takes a Polaroid snapshot of you and your hair is messed up or your clothes are hanging in a funny way, you see this instantly. The photo is self-explanatory. Similarly, when you construct a Tri-Astral picture, the strengths and weaknesses of your Adult, Child, and Parent become instantly delineated. The chart practically interprets itself.

The goal of this book is not only to teach you how to construct a Tri-Astral chart, but also to discover ways to work self-healing in those areas where healing may be needed. One of my reservations about much of psychological therapy is that it is purely verbal. We learn to talk about our problems but often miss the healing. I have had clients who have been in "talk" therapy for years and were still manifesting the same destructive behavior. Consider Karen's case. Karen was very articulate about why she had her problems, but still continued to manifest her negative behavior. However, by doing the diary exercises based on Tri-Astral astrology, she began to make substantial progress. Through her work with self-healing activities, she created meaningful internal dialogue and gave vent to her frustrations in a variety of hurt feelings. She achieved personal growth and maturity because she was willing to roll up her sleeves and address the opposing energies that were troubling her. As one client put it, "You gotta dig for the gold, all the time throwing out the dirt."

Tri-Astral astrology is also a useful tool for evaluating love relationships and the subpersonas involved. What are the respective strengths of each individual's personality? How will we interact? What games will he play? Is this person right for me? Can he give? Will she be competitive? Can he accept love? These questions are graphically answered by the Tri-Astral chart comparison techniques.

Actually, taking a look at the Tri-Astral personality charts of anyone in your life—your boss, friends, family, and others—can provide insight into their inner dynamics and give you keys to successful interaction. Having such a tool at your disposal can open new doors to understanding the people around you. Such a tool can bring new harmony into your life.

For the best results, use this book as a personal manual. Keep notes. Jot down what works and what doesn't work for you.

Note the exercises which gave you the greatest help, and which the least. Invent exercises of your own; personalize the process so that it works for you. Feel free to write and let me know about your progress, about how things are going for you. Think of me as an uncle who will listen with affection to you.

Finally, as you read this book, imagine that personal healing is like catching a fish when you are hungry. Now see that Tri-Astral astrology is like a net—a metaphorical net you can cast upon the waters of your mind. It enables you to draw living symbols from the depths of your consciousness. It will help you to catch that fish, personal healing, which will enable you to nourish and rejuvenate yourself. To do this, however, you must cast your net upon the water. You must work your process. You must tend your nets. Happy fishing!

Figure 3

John Lennon

Oct 9 1940   6:30 PM GMD
Liverpool   England
53N25   2W52
Oct 9 1940   17:30:00 GMT
Tropical   Koch   *True Node*

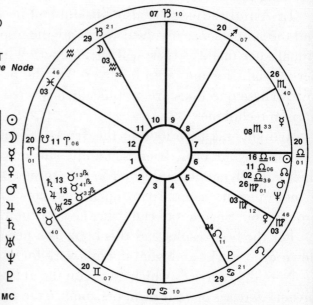

House Cusps

10th	07 ♑ 10	1st	20 ♈ 01
11th	29 ♑ 21	2nd	26 ♉ 40
12th	03 ♓ 46	3rd	20 ♊ 07

Personal Points

	R.A.M.C	277 48	
Medium Coeli	07 ♑ 10	Co Ascendant	12 ♈ 29
Ascendant	20 ♈ 01	Polar Ascendant	05 ♎ 22
Vertex	06 ♎ 26	Equatorial Ascendant	08 ♈ 30

Planets by Sign

1 Fire	
5 Earth	2 Cardinal
3 Air	6 Fixed
1 Water	2 Mutable

Planets by House

5 Life	
3 Substance	4 Angular
2 Relationships	3 Succedent
0 Endings	3 Cadent

	Long	Lat	Decl	R.A.
☉	16 ♎ 16 00	00 N 00	06 S 23	194 59
☽	03 ♒ 32	04 N 53	14 S 35	304 40
☿	08 ♏ 33	01 S 58	16 S 13	215 30
♀	03 ♍ 12	00 N 15	10 N 34	155 14
♂	02 ♎ 39	00 N 57	00 S 10	182 49
♃	13 ♉ 41 ℞	01 S 24	14 N 36	041 39
♄	13 ♉ 13 ℞	02 S 37	13 N 18	041 34
♅	25 ♉ 33 ℞	00 S 16	18 N 53	053 17
♆	26 ♍ 01	01 N 12	02 N 40	176 50
♇	04 ♌ 11	04 N 01	23 N 07	127 33
⚷	00 ♌ 33	06 S 46	13 N 24	121 16
♀	14 ♎ 06	09 N 38	03 N 19	196 42
⚸	16 ♌ 05	09 S 44	06 N 41	135 38
⚴	01 ♏ 27	05 N 24	06 S 53	211 11
⚳	12 ♌ 39	00 N 55	17 N 53	135 23

☊ **True 11 ♎ 06**   **Mean 10 ♎ 34 ℞**

Chapter One

The Magician tosses up a ball,
a second, then a third!
Now all three globes
hang suspended and pulsing,
dancing like one
before the enchanter's eye.

★ ☆ ☆ ☆ ☆ ☆ ★ ☆

The Three Spheres of Consciousness

Let the Games Begin!

Consciousness is a lot like juggling. The juggler is a mental magician deep within our psyche whose deft energy propels various visions before our inner eye. Different images, memories, and voices ascend into our awareness only to fade as other images and memories have their moment on the mind's center stage. Often these spheres of juggled consciousness are intense "tape" fragments from our past, common phrases that our parents used, scenes from how we were raised, or images from our early childhood recalling happy or sad moments. As this intense juggling of psychological material flashes before us, we can sense our emotions fluctuating as we relive old feelings. How well we can control the performance of this mental juggler determines our ability to focus our minds (be mindful), have self-control, and succeed in directing the growth of our lives.

Popular psychologists have studied this spontaneous fluctuation of mental material and call these juggled spheres of consciousness "ego states." Each of these ego states is organized by an implicit psychic attitude, a cohesive theme of concern or perspective that is the common denominator. While the general scope of these ego states may be quite diverse, the substance of their psychic attitudes seems to fall into three basic areas: parental attitudes and parental figures, rational or adult attitudes of objectivity in perceiving emotions and environment, and childhood memories and recollections that reflect key painful and pleasurable attitudes of our earliest experiences.

These three spheres of consciousness can be easily identified by referring to them simply as Parent, Adult, and Child, using capitals to show that they are specific proper nouns representing a psychological ego state. Through the metaphor of the juggler in our psyche we see mental health in terms of developing good balance and smooth control of the psychological energy flow between these three ego states. This harmony is manifested through the balanced expression of our personality.

Consider again the image of the juggler/magician and imagine him with his hands full, struggling to perform with the mental equivalent of a basketball, a soccer ball, and a bowling ball. Understandably, he is having trouble keeping them flowing in a balanced rhythm. If we look at these three mental balls as ego states, it is easy to see that the bowling ball ego state is "over-weighted" and is the cause of the juggler's difficulties. The trick is to determine whether the Parent, Adult, or Child is the bowling ball! Obviously, the ego state with the most psychological baggage is the source of the problems.

While the magician analogy is simple, it illustrates the key idea of balance. The task of self-therapy with this book or any psychological work with a counselor will center on discovering which mental state is overly weighted (has a lot of conflicting mental issues) and is causing personal pain. Yet the therapeutic job of evaluating these positive or negative influences can take some time and money because the process is slow and introspective.

Tri-Astral astrology can help you quickly understand the nature of your ego states and gain self-awareness, evolution, and self-healing. It does this by helping you determine the attitudes of the key mental players in your own inner games of love and life. Specifically, it graphically shows you the astrologically weighted make-up of your Parent, Adult, and Child.

A Tri-Astral chart will reveal a focused picture of the different positive and negative polarities within your personality. This will enable you to discover and then start working on these emotionally difficult areas. The goal is to heal your inner wounds, to clear away the debris of the past, and to initiate positive growth in the present. Love and its problems can be helped by understanding these areas of our psychological landscape. Stronger self-insights and improved communication skills are a part of this healing process.

The key to using this powerful self-help tool is to learn how easy it is to translate the three ego states of popular psychology into the astrological concepts of Tri-Astral analysis. The essential building block is to know the time, date, and place of your birth, or that of the individual you are analyzing. It is necessary to have accurate astrological data by having a chart prepared for you by an astrological service. If you want to create your own chart materials, you can follow the directions provided in Appendix A at the back of this book. This vital astrological information will provide you with the means for uncovering surprising psychological insights.

The first step in Tri-Astral astrology is to create a basic three-tier ego sphere diagram which will be the foundation for all other evaluations. An ego sphere is the Tri-Astral equivalent of an ego state. A focusing planet is used to symbolize each of the three ego spheres and enables astrological information to be used in a new way. Saturn and its sign represents the Parent, the Sun and its sign the Adult, and the Moon and its sign the Child. Now, let's see how it works.

Get to Know Your Neighbor in Spirit: John Lennon

Imagine that John Lennon has moved to your neighborhood; you want to know what he is like and how best to strike up a friendship with him. You can hear him practicing his guitar and he seems like a person you would like to get to know. You decide to construct a Tri-Astral chart to gain perspective.

The first step is to get John's birth data. John was a Libra and was not shy about giving out his birthday—October 9, 1940, 06:30 pm, BST, Liverpool. From this you can erect his traditional natal chart (figure 3).

John Lennon's birth chart is a complex challenge for even the most experienced astrologer. There are so many complicated configurations that it is a puzzle how even to begin an interpretation. However, let's forego traditional astrology and see how we can pull information from John's horoscope to start constructing the three circles of a Tri-Astral chart.

The key is to take the positions of Saturn, the Sun, and the Moon in the natal chart and highlight them as John's basic ego spheres—Parent, Adult, and Child (figure 4). These focus planets show us the first step in developing his Tri-Astral chart, and even these bare bones have a rewarding tale to tell. This simple diagram represents the archetypal energy each ego sphere is generating. Each planet's primary psychic attitude is filtered by the specific sign in which it resides. The combined energy of planet and sign is the basic essence of the ego sphere. The three spheres show the basics of personality structure.

Let's go through this basic three-tier format to reveal how much we already know about John Lennon. John's Parent planet, Saturn, is in Taurus. This means that John's Parent ego sphere has a basically stubborn, realistic, and materialistic attitude. This will give his Parent great persistence and stamina. Taurus is aligned with (or ruled by) Venus and likes pleasure, wealth, and possessions. Whether or not there is money, there may be a fear of poverty. (Remember John's famous quip, "I'm down to my last 50,000 quid.") There is a lot of creative and sexual energy in Taurus to which Saturn gives form and content. Creative projects can lead to peace of mind. There is a definite tendency to be extremely possessive with loved ones, and jealousy can be a problem. There is a quality of having to see something to believe it—the earthy quality of Taurus and the structuring quality of Saturn make for a person who likes to "see it in black and white."

John's Adult or Sun ego sphere is in Libra. Libra is nothing if not charming, artistic, and diplomatic. There is tremendous artistic potential, for the love of beauty is an important part of the Libran personality. Harmonious and looking for a good time, the Libra loves the good life of parties and social events. Romance is paramount to a Libra—the world loves lovers, and Libras love. There is an ability to work in partnerships, both in work and marriage. Judgment is sharp, for Libra is the balancing scales, though sometimes the scales wobble and some indecisiveness can be experienced. There is an added artistic feature in that both John's Sun and Saturn, Adult and Parent, are ruled by Venus. This adds to the artistic temperament and need to create.

John's Child or Moon sphere is in Aquarius. This Child is emotionally detached, and there is the feeling of being an observer, of being ahead of one's time. Personal originality may cut you off from the herd. This Child is very liberated sexually. The creative energy is strong. Idealistic and broad-minded, this person has strong humanitarian feelings of wanting to embrace the world. This Child can change his or her mind suddenly and become cold and emotionally distant. The mother of this Child is often unusual, if not an outright nonconformist.

These three ego sphere descriptions give us the basic framework for understanding our new neighbor, John Lennon. Even at this fundamental

Figure 4

John Lennon's basic ego spheres chart

13 ♉
**SATURN
PARENT**

16 ♎
**SUN
ADULT**

3 ♒
**MOON
CHILD**

level of personality study we can discern the charming, dramatic, artistic, and humanitarian qualities that endeared John to his fans. Yet also note the qualities of stubbornness, isolation, depression, and neediness that formed the shadow side of his personality.

A more complete Tri-Astral analysis of John Lennon's personal psychology will be created in the next chapter when we add the rest of the planets to John's ego sphere chart. Consider the three circles of the ego spheres to be a skeleton for which the planets will later supply the flesh. In combination, they give us a complete and dramatic visual representation of the inner dynamics of this famous musician.

How to Create a First Step, "Bare Bones" Tri-Astral Chart

Following the example used with John Lennon, get out your own astrological chart or that of a friend you are interested in knowing better. Locate Saturn, the Sun, and the Moon and make a three-ring Parent, Adult, and Child diagram based on noting Saturn and its sign, the Sun and its sign, and the Moon and its sign.

Directions:

1. Using the information in Appendix A, obtain a natal chart generated by a computer service or create your own using reference books on astrology at a local library. Locate your Saturn and its sign. Place it in the Parent sphere in the blank ego spheres chart (figure 5). (You may want to photocopy this page to have several blank charts with which to experiment.) Be sure to include its degree and sign (i.e., Saturn at 13° Taurus for John Lennon). Then look up the Sun and put it in the center circle along with its degree and sign. Finally, put the Moon in the Child circle with its degree and sign.

2. Turn to Appendix B in the back of this book and find the definitions for the major archetypes:

   Look up the meaning of Saturn and its sign.

   Look up the meaning of the Sun and its sign.

   Look up the meaning of the Moon and its sign.

Figure 5

Blank ego spheres chart to use as a worksheet

3. Write them down in a notebook. Respond to where you agree and disagree with the general meanings given in the appendix. Fine-tune these definitions by adding your own insights into the meanings of the ego spheres. Be sure to ground your observations with concrete examples such as, "This Parent would strike a child," or "This Adult is warm and would give great hugs."

4. Parent work: Choose an environment where you can relax without interruption and let your mind drift back over the events of your life. As you remember various situations and monitor the different types of interior monologues, pick out the phrases that you most remember hearing from your parents. My advice is to get a small tape recorder and tape your thoughts as they come to you. Review the tape, edit your comments, and write down those which you sense to be significant. How do these old thought patterns affect you now?

5. Adult work: Who was an adult role model for you? Was it a parent, a relative, someone in a friend's family? Maybe it was a sports figure, a public figure, or a film star. Take some time and list key adults in your life. Have you changed adult heroes often? Write these thoughts down.

6. Child work: What kinds of play did you experience as a child? Take some time to remember your earliest memories and what you liked to do. Again, use a tape recorder, if you can, to capture your memories. Who determined what you played? What was fun for you? Who did you play with? Did you have a favorite teddy bear or toy? Who antagonized you the most? What was your favorite food? Write a summary of the highs and lows of your Child's experience.

At this point you have successfully created a basic Tri-Astral diagram, used the major archetypes to determine the general disposition of each ego state, and have personalized it with your own comments about the prevailing attitudes of your Parent, Adult, and Child. Finally, you have responded to the exercises dealing with personal monitoring, thus beginning to build a meaningful notebook which will enhance your healing process.

You are now ready to proceed to the next level of the Tri-Astral chart construction, that of putting the planets in—which provides a meaningful, simple, and accurate means to weigh the spheres. Or, you might say, to determine which is the power sphere. Remember, the goal is to know where your personal strengths and weakness are, where you are healthy, and where you have toxicity. Stay grounded in your reflections by keeping a notebook of your thoughts, dreams, and memories as you work through this book. You'll reap the rewards that await you when you use this process for insight and growth. We are all explorers in the quest for self-discovery.

Figure 6

CONJUNCTION
0°
(+ or - 7°)

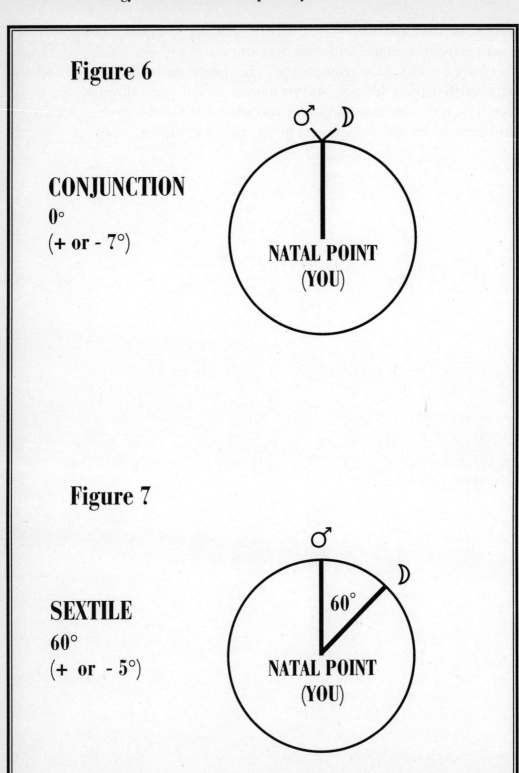

NATAL POINT
(YOU)

Figure 7

SEXTILE
60°
(+ or - 5°)

NATAL POINT
(YOU)

Chapter Two

See the Magician high on the wire
juggling three different balls
above a cheering crowd.
His skill is practiced;
his fingers know each shape and weight,
his quick, sure wrists adjust the toss
as they arc in an even flow.
This momentum is a balance all its own.

★ ★ ☆ ★ ★ ☆ ★ ★

Putting the Self on the Scales

Who Carries the Weight Around Here?

No matter what your personal Sun sign is, try to approach the Tri-Astral method of weighing the ego spheres by focusing your mind on the symbolic principle of the balancing scales. With our "Libra cap" on, so to speak, our task is to learn how to survey, measure, and evaluate the relative personality strengths of an individual based on an assessment of the relative potency of the three ego spheres, Parent, Adult, and Child.

This disciplined and evaluative overview will open up the deeper personality structures, revealing the psyche's hidden energy interactions which form the inner composition of the whole self. To be accurate in this undertaking, we must be fair, we must be compassionate, and we must be objective. With faith in both our reasoned and intuitive processes, we will seek to probe and understand the workings of the inner psyche. Developing this balanced insight is the first step toward healing ourselves or in reaching out with understanding to another.

Our tools for developing this deep psychological/spiritual perception lie in discerning the dynamics of basic planetary aspects, those significant geometric angles formed by the planets in the natal chart. Don't let the technical sound of this language bother you. It is as simple as cutting up a pizza. Specifically, we must learn to discern the nature of the angular relationships of each natal planet to the key ego sphere planets of the Sun, the Moon, and Saturn. These aspects are fundamental for an evaluation of the ego spheres.

A good approach is to think of an aspect as a geometric piece of pie involving two planets and the earth. The angle the two planets on the rim create at the apex, or the earthly point of the piece of pie, indicates the type of dynamic energy or psychological qualities this planetary pair will generate.

There are six angles or aspects which form the most important pieces of the pie. These classic angles can be used to identify how planetary/psychological energy manifests in the psyche. Learn these aspects and their meanings as faithfully as you studied traffic signs to pass your driver's test. Like traffic signs, aspects are astrological signals that tell us of the nature of the psychological interior. And if one must travel that interior road, or journey inward with another, we will benefit by what our aspect map tells us about the terrain and where the passage might be difficult.

Aspects and Personal Dynamics

To illustrate these six major aspects and their importance, let's consider the six basic angles between the Moon and Mars (figures 6–11). The Moon, of course, is the Child ego sphere, symbolizing our emotions, nurturing, and feelings. Mars is a planet of our deep drives for survival, for sexuality, for hunting, fighting, defending, and competing. How these two energy sources interact is determined by their relative natal positions to one another. Let's take a look.

Conjunction

We start with a conjunction (figure 6), which is not a piece of pie, but a dot, for the planets are standing side by side, within 0–9° of each other. If these planets were people, they could smell each other's perfume and cologne, and know who's bigger than whom. Conjunctions are close planetary contacts, and, like people, some planets seem to get along better at close quarters than others.

For the Moon and Mars this conjunction position is a little too close; there is a great amount of tension, emotions run high, and feelings and tempers can be passionate. It would be easier for the Moon if Venus were next to it. Venus is a more harmonious planet and not so likely to pique the Moon's emotions.

Mars conjunct Moon is a little like having a big brother around. There is always an undertone that something may happen. Tempers can flare. And when Mars, our metaphorical big brother, isn't out trapping bugs, he's picking on the soft feminine Moon to harass its temperament. It's his way. There is a Walt Disney naturalist movie on bears which points out that bears express affection with a slap. This is Moon/Mars. The Inner Child has to deal with wide-ranging temperaments and, potentially, even abuse.

Sextile

Now see what happens as the Moon moves to the 60° or sextile position (figure 7). This aspect looks like a piece of pie. There is a playfulness to this position—the planets are apart now, but still close enough to appreciate this new distance. There is more freedom of movement, more subtleties. Mars is not smothering the Moon, as in the conjunction. The Inner Child is not restricted by the temperament and energies of Mars. Big brother is not sharing your space. There is room to be an individual.

Square

When the Moon and Mars are shifted to make an aspect of 90° they form the square position (figure 8), a very dynamic and powerful angle. Squares promote movement—the energies of the planets need to change; there is an inner pull that must be followed. In the conjunction the planets are almost too close, in the sextile there is a playful exploration of freedom, but in the square there *must* be action. The position is not static; something must give.

The square was considered to be a bad aspect by ancient astrologers. Being in the employ of kings, noblemen and wealthy merchants, these astrologers had clients who resisted change. Thus the square, the 90° aspect, was viewed with suspicion and considered dangerous because it threatened the status quo. Today's astrologers view squares with a different eye. Squares are the yeast in the dough, the doers, the active motivators that make things happen, that challenge. If squares bring about change, then that change is undoubtedly needed.

What modern astrology does advocate is "square control"—identify where squares are working in your Tri-Astral personality map, and understand that where there are squares there is a potential for volatility. It is prudent to give that area special attention. For example, the Moon square Mars is a strong

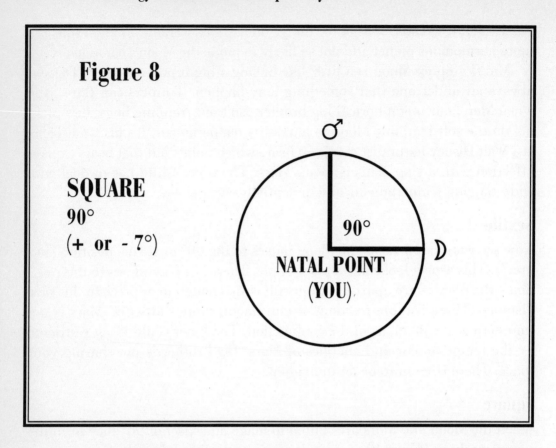

Figure 8

SQUARE
90°
(+ or - 7°)

♂

90°

NATAL POINT
(YOU)

☽

aspect; it gives the personality the "inner warriors" that Robert Bly writes about in *Iron John*. One with this aspect can summon up the inner warriors to protect oneself and others and has the drive to compete, to struggle, and to survive. But one also has to be sure that these warriors don't go off on a hair-trigger, that one doesn't get mad over little things, and that one's temper does not get out of control.

Trine

The 120° point, or trine, is often the most loved aspect (figure 9). You can feel the ease in planetary and personal relationships where this equilateral energy is present. The dynamic of the square is gone and the angle of the trine makes for a sense of flow. The ancient astrologers loved the trine as much as they worried about the square. The trine is often considered the "great goody giver," bringing harmony and expansion to the status quo. Modern astrologers have toned down this adulation of the trine to a more realistic evaluation. Trines represent harmony, easy flow, and often a productive and constructive manifestation of latent energies. However, trines can represent being soft, relying on natural talents, and not digging deep and developing real fortitude.

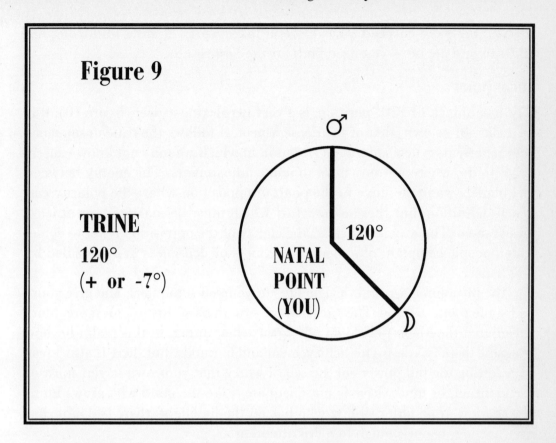

Figure 9

TRINE
120°
(+ or -7°)

NATAL
POINT
(YOU)

120°

The Moon/Mars trine represents a wonderful blending of the energies of the Inner Child with the instinctive survival hunches of Mars. These people make for great lovers and good diplomats. They don't seem to grow old as quickly as other mortals and are sensitive in their emotional outlook.

"Where's the catch?" you ask. The catch is in motivation. The square can push; the trine can make you lazy. It represents the things you do most easily, and while this is wonderful, with trines there is a tendency to be passive about our talents, to not practice enough, to rely on innate skills and not push to new levels. Consider it similar to lovers who fall into an easy romance, don't work on their love, and separate when a real challenge comes along. Or it is like an social fad that only goes so far before it fails to amuse and falls by the wayside.

Trine management is needed. An individual must apply discipline to his or her talents. How many times have you seen an individual who was a good musician (Moon trine Neptune, to mention just one aspect that could apply here) who could have been a great musician, yet refused to practice, to work? Such reliance on a natural ability is not managing a trine, not nurturing an innate ability. To succeed takes more: it takes work. Squares and trines are like salt and pepper—you need both for the best results.

Inconjunct

The inconjunct, or 150° position, is a very perplexing aspect (figure 10). It is in a class of its own, that of the dense aspect. It follows the trine in sequence and represents a new emotional situation in which we may not know exactly what to do, where we may have to make adjustments. The energy between the planets wants to move to the point of opposition where the polarity can reach definition, but there is new turf which must be mastered, or at least transversed. The way is not clear; the clarity of the opposition is yet to come. Often people complain of a mental heaviness or denseness in areas ruled by this aspect.

The inconjunct aspect is a signal to cut yourself some slack and give yourself some room to grow. The "gravity" of situations seems to pull more. Mars inconjunct the Moon people do not "own" their anger. In this realm beyond the trine there is a desire for achievement and harmony, but there is also a fear of asserting the full powers of the self, a worry that your own anger, spirit of competition, or inner drive is not adequate. Like the child who grows up in the shadow of an older sibling who has all the limelight, there is doubt that your feelings count enough to merit attention.

While the feelings indicated by this Moon/Mars inconjunct are significant, it takes time for the Inner Child to learn how to accept the validity of these feelings—to "own" them. For many this is a most difficult aspect since its psychological dimensions are so inwardly focused and subtle in the need for adjustments.

Opposition

The opposition, or 180° angle, now has our example planets, the Moon and Mars, facing each other (figure 11). The pie is divided in half. The opposition represents the zenith, the greatest distance possible between two planets. You might find it easy to remember by calling the opposition the "face-off." In this position two planets face each other, one on each side, as if pulling the Earth in two directions. This pull brings into sharpest focus the boundaries of the two planetary energies, revealing the nature of their polarity. The key to handling oppositions is to learn to bring things together, to discover ways to resolve these two polarities. For example, when the Moon and Mars are in opposition there is the need to bring into synthesis the Inner Child's playful

Figure 10

INCONJUNCT
150°
(+ or - 5°)

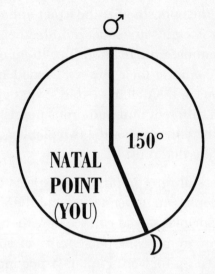

Figure 11

OPPOSITION
180°
(+ or - 7°)

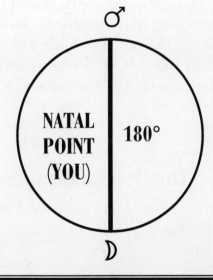

and sensitive nature with the aggressive and sexual energies of Mars. This means learning how to be sensitive and still stick up for oneself; how to be playful, but not hurtful; how to enjoy sex; and how to appreciate the creature comforts of life.

Note that the opposition is the exact opposite of the conjunction in which the planetary energies are squeezed together. In the conjunction, the slower planet will dominate the relationship. In an opposition, however, the planets have room to manifest their powers. Comedians, for example, often have several oppositions in their charts—that's what gives them their ability to look at life from such different and humorous points of view. The focus of the opposition is that the difference of the two planets can be clearly manifested, which creates a tension that must be resolved.

The successful interpretation of aspects in weighing ego spheres comes through developing an understanding of these elemental angles, and digesting these basic principles so you can see how they work with the different planets. This is the way to have the personality of yourself, your lover, friends, and coworkers open up for you. Planets aspecting the ego spheres supply all the clues to understanding how a personality is structured—where a person is strong, where weak, and where he or she hurts or shines. See Appendix C for an analysis of the meaning of each of the major planetary aspects and the ego spheres. This will give you some grounding in the meaning of the aspects upon which you can build.

Remember, the reason for studying aspects is to learn to weigh the ego spheres to determine the psychological baggage at each level. This is the very basis of astro-analysis and the springboard to insights. Make notes of your own and consult with other astrological resources. Develop real experience with these aspects. They are the building blocks of all astrological work. See how your own analysis relates to what you will read in this book, then learn to adjust the combined input. Make it a habit to look at a chart from several points of view. Because we are all different, we need to be flexible and make adjustments when needed. This will make for accuracy.

The Weighted Value of Aspects

Now that you can see and understand some of the basics of aspects, let's turn to the next important step in this weighing process: the ranking of the aspects in three categories.

Color Code Aspect

red	Hard:	
	Conjunctions 0°, Squares 90°, Oppositions 180°	
blue	Flowing:	
	Sextiles 60°, Trines 120°	
green	Dense or adjusting:	
	Inconjuncts 150°	

The trick is to take the natal chart of the individual you are analyzing and look at what is called the planetary aspectarian, which is "astrologese" for a "list of aspects." Return to John Lennon's chart (figure 3). Note the aspectarian, a grid or list of all the aspects each planet makes in John's chart. Look for the aspects of the planets to the ego spheres—Sun, Moon, and Saturn. The computer has done all the calculations and conveniently labels and lists them for you. Getting a prepared chart with an aspectarian can save you a lot of time. However, it is possible to do this by hand by using the planetary positions and your knowledge of the degrees of the different aspects.

It is important to understand the concept of orbs when looking at aspects, especially if you are preparing your own chart from the information in an ephemeris. The key idea of orbs is similar to horseshoes: if it is close enough, it counts. You will not find too may planetary aspects in your chart that are exact—that is, exactly 60°, 90°, 120°, etc.

The key is to allow an orb, which means that if the Moon and Mars are 85° apart, they are within orb, close enough to 90° to be considered a square. Got it? Allow a 9° orb for conjunctions, oppositions, squares, and trines. Allow a 5° orb for sextiles and inconjuncts. If the planets are not "within orb," they are not considered an aspect and don't count in the analysis work in this method. Consider the example of horseshoes: a ringer is an exact orb; shoes that fall within the distance of the peg equal to that of the open "U" of the shoe are "counters," or within orb. All others do not count in a tally because they do not "measure up." The shoe doesn't fit. In other words, close not only counts in horseshoes, but also in astrological aspects.

You now know about aspects and how they are classified as hard, flowing, or adjusting. The key is balance. If an ego sphere has more hard aspects, it will be overly aggressive and more traumatized sometimes because of battle scars. If there are more flowing aspects, the ego sphere will be talented, but perhaps lazy.

If there are more dense or adjusting aspects, the ego sphere will lack self-confidence, adding a constant worry modality to the system. This quick summary will be broadened in the chapters to come. For now, as a beginner you know the rudiments about aspects and their psychological indicators.

Putting It All Together—A Picture Worth A Thousand Shrinks

Our next step is to show you how to take the natal aspects that are within orb and attach them to the chart of the three ego states, finishing the Tri-Astral astrological chart and creating an evaluative map. This visual aid will present an analysis so striking that patterns will seem to leap from the page to your eye. The ego sphere with the most aspects is the most charged with mental and emotional energy.

Ready? To illustrate how this works, let's look at John Lennon's chart again. We already know the position of John's planetary ego states (review the sparse skeleton in figure 4). The next step in creating a complete astro-analysis chart is to add the planets that are in aspect (within orb) to John's Sun, Moon, and Saturn. Look at John's natal chart again (figure 3). You have just learned that the aspectarian at the bottom of the chart shows all of John's aspects. You need only pick out the major aspects to the Sun, Moon, and Saturn. There are three areas to consider:

1. John's Saturn has two hard aspects: a Mercury opposition and a Jupiter conjunction. There is one dense inconjunct to the Sun.

2. John's Sun has two dense inconjunct aspects: one to Saturn and one to Jupiter.

3. John's Moon has three flowing aspects: trines with Mars, Neptune, and Uranus; and two hard aspects: an opposition to Pluto and a square to his ascendant; and one dense adjusting aspect to Venus.

Weighing the Spheres

When we attach this information to John's Tri-Astral chart it takes on a shape of its own (figure 12). Note that all the planets which make an aspect with an ego state are attached with a line and symbol representing the nature of the aspect (trine, square, etc). For example, Mars is represented by a line and a triangle representing a trine to the Child ego state or the Moon.

One of the key reasons for using a Tri-Astral chart is that you can get a quick overview of the astrological/psychological makeup of an individual. Our task in determining the strength or weight of the chart is to find which ego sphere has the most aspects, and what kind of aspects they are.

It is instantly obvious that John Lennon's Inner Child/Moon in Aquarius is the most aspected or heavily weighted ego state. This sphere fueled this great Beatle's success, and the inner trials he went through can be understood in a large part by the dynamics of his Inner Child. Let's look at each of John's ego states as an example of how quickly Tri-Astral astrology can cut to the heart of the matter.

There are six aspects to John's Child ego sphere. The three flowing trines from Mars, Neptune, and Uranus give John his ability to be playful, to have great stamina, to love the unusual, the creative, the bizarre. The trine to Neptune in particular gives him a great fantasy life, a dreamer mentality, an interest in alternative states of consciousness and mind-altering substances, as well as visionary utopian inclinations. The trine to Uranus makes him almost compulsively creative, a person that hates to repeat himself, a risk-taker.

The hard aspects tell us another story. The Pluto opposition to the Moon tells of a deep problem with women, with his mother, and of possibly traumatic problems related to the mother. Certainly John's feelings of isolation when his mother left him home alone during the German bombing of England is represented by this dark aspect. John tried to resolve this in his song, "Mother." The Moon's square to the ascendant adds a deep need for compulsive play in John's life. It is as if after all the early trauma, he must make up for lost time that he will never regain.

Most interesting is the Moon inconjunct Venus. This aspect shows how unsure our famous Beatle was in his view of women, and the true nature of his own feelings about being lovable. John actually had quite a bit of doubt about his ability to be loved, at least for being loved for himself alone, and not for his many achievements. The desire to be in show business, to be a musical sensation, in some ways shows John's need for something to attract a woman. Yet there is also the desire not to be loved as a star, a performer, but for his ability to understand intimacy and for his intrinsic worth. There is the gnawing doubt that he is not lovable without his ability to impress.

Clearly John's Moon or Child ego sphere is a complex contradiction of great creative talent, trauma, and inner insecurities. It is the driving force of his primal energy. More planetary contacts and energy are active here than in any other ego sphere, so the Child's impact on the personality has to be very dynamic. Looking at John Lennon's life, it is apparent that his Inner Child was a large player; it had the lion's share of John's psychological energy. He and Yoko were "Two Virgins," two children, and the world media was their playpen.

John's Parent/Saturn ego sphere has two hard aspects, indicating that he would be hard on his Inner Child. He would want to be tough and focused in unusual ways. The opposition of Mercury to Saturn gave John his big mouth, his ability to talk rough, denounce the old order, to announce that the group is more "popular than Jesus," and to create that strange little book, *John Lennon in his Own Write.*

This Mercury opposition not only made John a tough talker, the quip master, but it also made him a writer, a writer who had to deal with the reality of pop formulas, of learning this format and transcending it. There is also an anti-authoritarian bite to this aspect which made him question the rules of our culture.

The conjunction of Jupiter to Saturn, the Parent ego sphere, shows John's great need to prove himself in a grand, "Jupiterian" manner. Jupiter is the planet of expansion, of seeking to shoot high the arrows of ambition. Saturn is the critic, always forcing one to prove oneself—to put up or shut up. For John, this meant great ambition and the driving need to be somebody to the world. It was not enough to have the desire to go into music, John's Parent was pushing him to make it big, to show the world that he was somebody. It wasn't enough to be a "wannabe" in a pop band. John wanted to really prove himself, to make real (Saturn) his ambition (Jupiter).

John's Adult/Sun is his weakest ego sphere. Torn between a powerful, talented, emotionally traumatized Child and a critical Parent, the Adult sphere is insecure, a state which is symbolized by the inconjunctions of Saturn and Jupiter. For John, being one of the leaders of the peace movement, fighting authority, talking tough about the war, proclaiming the message of love, love, love, was easy. When this Beatle-person grew up—became a parent himself, a solo artist, had a wife (Yoko)—now what? It was a difficult transition into the Adult sphere, one that led him to become a "house-husband," withdrawing for long periods of time "watching the world go 'round." We will never know how John would have solved the riddles of the inconjuncts to his Adult, for he was gunned down just as he was about to emerge, just when he had gotten a handle on his own maturity, his own fatherhood, and his recovered and transformed feelings about his inner self.

This brief look at John Lennon illustrates two of the many uses of a Tri-Astral analysis of an individual. First, it shows how quick, accurate, succinct, and easy to interpret this method can be. With just a basic framework in astrology you are able to follow the astro-psychology. Second, it gives information in a usable form that can provide insights on how to deal with a specific individual, and tactics one might use for success in a relationship. To illustrate this point, let's return to the astro-analysis of John Lennon (review figure 12).

How to Meet John

What might be the best way to approach John? What would be a good way to get on the good side of our new neighbor? The first task is to decide which of the ego spheres might be most receptive to this venture. Certainly John's Parent is too verbal, too combative, too tough; the Saturn has no soft aspects. The Adult is too uncommitted—a Libra Sun with two inconjuncts means John waffles.

This leaves the Child as the best ego sphere to approach. The Moon's trines to Mars, Neptune, and Uranus tell the story. The best way to approach John is in a playful, young-at-heart way, take him by surprise, and make him laugh. Amazingly enough, this is exactly how Yoko chose to meet John. One wonders if she hadn't consulted an astrologer. What did Yoko do? She covered herself with a bag and approached John as he was previewing an art show. This playful act delighted the Child in John and he became immediately interested in Yoko. Truly an example of the right approach at the right time.

Synopsis of the Steps for Generating a Tri-Astral Analysis Chart

Let's review the process for creating and evaluating the Tri-Astral analysis chart as well as giving some helpful hints as to how to use this chart as a stepping stone to psychological discovery.

Follow the sequence given below:

1. Get the correct date, time, and place of birth of yourself or the individual for whom you are creating the chart.
2. Have an astrological computer center compute an exact chart for you, or use the information from library references to hand-generate the data needed.

Figure 12

John Lennon's Tri-Astral chart

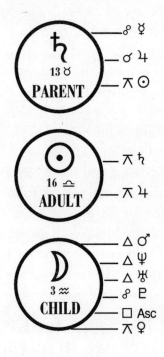

3. Create a "bare bones" chart with the three rings stacked perpendicularly with the sign and degree of Saturn, the Sun, and the Moon as the three ego spheres.

4. Look up the meaning of each ego sphere planet in its sign in Appendix B. This gives a basic feel for each ego sphere in its "pure" or unaspected climate.

5. Write down all the planets making major aspects (trine, sextile, square, conjunction, inconjunction, and opposition) with each of the ego sphere planets. Attach those planets graphically to the appropriate ego sphere in the astro-analysis chart.

6. Look up the meaning of these planetary aspects in Appendix C. Consider the distribution of the aspects to the ego spheres, then evaluate and rank them according to the hard, soft, or adjusting qualities that are indicated. It is easy to see which has the most planets aspecting it. Good indicators to begin your study of the ego sphere are:

   Which has the most aspects?

   Which has the least?

   Which has the most hard aspects?

   Which has the most soft aspects?

   Which has the most adjusting aspects?

These questions and ones you create will supply the basis for a realistic evaluation of the strengths and weakness of the ego spheres and will pave the way to an insightful evaluation of the individual's character, such as was done with the example of John Lennon.

Getting in Personal Touch With the Ego Spheres

Now that you have the chart laid out before you and can see how ego spheres are weighed according to the aspects to the planets, take some time to really analyze and think about this chart. Go through each of the aspects and planets involved and see how they connect. Get a feel for each aspect. For example, if there are squares to Saturn, feel and hear the voice of the demanding Parent. After you have done this, try the following method.

Approach each ego sphere and do a modified form of psycho-drama. Pretend that you are the ego sphere and act it out. Imagine how it feels to be that

Parent, Adult, or Child. Personify it in some way. Make the sphere a pillow, a picture, a lamp shade, something on which to focus as you begin to talk out loud to that part of the chart. Ask questions of it and then imagine how it would answer. Remember to do this out loud, actually talking to your person-ification of the chart symbol and acting out its reply. This may feel a little awkward at first. You may need to adjust a little to talk to a lamp as if it were a Parent. But remember, this imaginative dialogue can open you up to great insights. Your own subconscious and higher intuitive levels will be called into service and the results will be rewarding. You will find yourself saying things that will amaze you.

If the chart you are working on is your own, I strongly recommend that you tape record these sessions of dialoguing with the ego spheres. You will dis-cover that in your psycho-drama things will come up. These issues will moti-vate you to know more about specific psychological conditions, even surprising memories of events that you may have forgotten. One of my clients rediscovered by voice-dialoguing with her Child that she had run away from home once, and had walked across town to her favorite aunt's house. This awakened her to how much denial she had about the truly traumatic rela-tionship she had with her mother when she was a young child. Working through that pain rather than living the false fantasy that her childhood had been "idyllic" enabled her to get a realistic grasp on herself.

It is also important that you include in your notebook (suggested at the end of Chapter 1) any new insights or memories that this form of psycho-drama produces. As these notebook notations grow and you continue to work with the ego spheres, big pieces to the puzzle of personality will fall into place for you. Doing this notebook work is like mining ore—the more you dig, the more nuggets you get. The ore is not going to jump out of the mine and into your lap. You have to work for it.

Another important step is to develop an awareness of how your ego spheres react during your day-to-day activities. If you are studying yourself, be aware of your words, your tone of voice, gestures, actions, and thoughts. Develop the habit of asking yourself from time to time, "What was the root of that behavior? Which ego sphere was talking?" It is important to be aware of your own programming. As your awareness grows, your ability to grow and change becomes more positive.

If you are studying your prospective romantic partner, you may want to see if you can tell when the different ego spheres are functioning in his or her personality. When is the Child active? What provokes the Parent? How mature is the Adult? Where does the anger come from? Observations like this will enable you to see if growth with this person is possible; if a relationship is something that could be worked out. More specific comparison techniques will be given in later chapters. And like a good musician, you must practice your listening and playing skills.

You may discover some tricky areas. The next chapter will illustrate some particularly challenging configurations of the ego spheres. Remember, the journey to discover the self in this life reflects the greater journey of the soul. We are all travelers on a greater highway. One of my clients once wrote:

> *The game is so real to us*
> *If a game is what it is.*
> *It would be nice to know the score*
> *In terms not etched in pain.*
> *I long for when it was*
> *Child's play.*

I always liked this, enough to include it here. And let us not forget that in the context of life as a game, there is an umpire—time—who keeps us going with a simple cry: "Play ball!" If play ball we must, let's learn to do our best. Let's look at some problems that must be flagged. We will discuss these in Chapter 3.

Figure 13

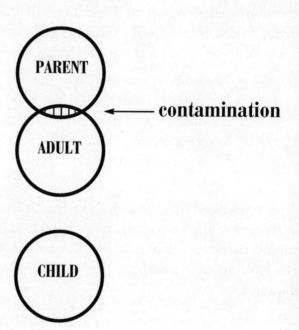

**PARENT
CONJUNCT ADULT
SATURN ♂ SUN**

Chapter Three

See the Juggler's electrifying skills,
tossing the spheres, one—two—three,
now catching them behind his back,
now bouncing them on his head—
Wait! One is stuck to his nose!
It stays fast, he can't get it off!
Since birth he's struggled with this.
It spurs his skill and ingenuity.

★ ★ ☆ ★ ★ ☆ ★ ☆

Overlapping Spheres: Toxic Turf

When Selves Collide

"Too close for comfort" is one way of expressing everyone's need for necessary space, both psychological and physical. As the old saying goes, "don't fence me in." We all need territory—our own room, apartment, locker, desk, or parking space—that reflects our need for an environment that is vital for self-expression. These are areas where we can express our individuality, where we can push for elbow room. In understanding the psychological dimension space takes on an added meaning, for we need space to grow. "Don't crowd me" is the way we express this deep need for room to discover ourselves.

If, for example, your parents "crowded" you, there is a good chance that you didn't feel as free to be yourself. You had to develop methods of dealing with your parents, and you had to use a lot of your psyche's energy in dealing with how they made you feel about yourself. Too much closeness can be toxic, causing you great pain. Tri-Astral astrology puts special emphasis on noting this need for individual space. Some situations reflected in planetary positions are breeding grounds for negative energy and bring up unique problems for growth.

In looking at the ego spheres, it is important to note how much space the planets symbolizing these spheres have between each other. If any combination of the Sun, Moon, or Saturn are in conjunction (within 7°), then the planets are so close together that a Tri-Astral astrologer would call them "contaminated" ego spheres. This is a toxic condition that affects the clarity of boundaries between different states of consciousness and distorts a person's ability to individuate.

There are six basic types of contaminated ego spheres, each with its own characteristics. While they occur infrequently, their extremely strong influence on the dynamics of the personality cannot be underestimated. The general rule to remember is that the slower planet dominates. Saturn dominates the Sun and the Moon, and the Sun dominates the Moon.

Figure 13 shows how the Saturn/Sun conjunction is graphically depicted in the language of ego spheres. The Adult (Sun) is dominated by the Parent (Saturn). These individuals are always trying to live up to a very strict hidden agenda in their minds, one set down by the demands of a Parent who has seriously affected the Adult's ability to grow in independence and originality. The concept of Parent and Adult are blurred; there are no boundaries. The Parent's mindset misdirects the Adult away from maturity and rational thinking. Instead, the Parent advances its own plans, complicating the Adult's world with its restrictive themes and agendas based on bias, opinions, and prejudice with no regard to rational discussion or behavior. Here is the Adult who is always too hard on him or herself and others. The Adult finds it difficult to have any fun, because the Parent ego sphere is taking charge and the Adult fun must follow the rules laid down by Saturn. The result is an uptight person who, when not busy putting him or herself down, is busy pointing out the flaws of others. These people will rain on your parade as easily as they rain on their own.

It takes a lot of effort to work through this kind of toxic Parent experience. People can become crippled by guilt. They feel they should work harder and get more done. They feel unworthy unless they are working and worrying for two.

If there is a hard Neptune aspect to this conjunction, the individual can sometimes fall into compulsive attempts at "self-medication" through mind-altering drugs like alcohol, nicotine, or barbiturates. Or they might be compulsively clean, not drinking or smoking, but abstaining in such a flagrant way as to be a martyr, their "purity" always distracting from any kind of a good time. They make their good habits a real pain in the neck to others. This holier-than-thou attitude gives them a perverse pleasure. But are they happy? No, only momentarily less guilty.

The first thing these people need to discover is that there is a difference between being an Adult and acting out the parental demands that were made upon them in their childhood years. Starting with those early years and working forward, they need to unwind the restrictive mental cord with which their parents tied them. The goal is to start acting out patterns which allow play and delight, emotions the Parent repressed and subverted.

For this individual, love is often seen as something earned. Affection is a reward, if it is experienced at all. All this needs to be unlearned and then restructured by creating a better self-image. While this is not an easy task, the best exercise is to write a biography and retell the story of your life. Pay particular attention to ways that rules were introduced and why. Be open to new ways of reframing the concept of self. Begin a dialogue with your dreams through a dream log. Start a diary. This process will bring change through insight. There is something about the process of self-searching on paper that leads to discovery.

Kari

Figure 14 is the Tri-Astral chart for a client of mine whose name has been changed to protect her anonymity. We will call her Kari. Kari came from strong German parents who barely escaped from the pogroms and death camps. Kari was very strictly raised. Love was doled out on a merit basis. She had an older brother who did everything right, who earned great grades and became a successful lawyer. Kari's own opinion of herself was very poor. She was brilliant, a good student, a hard worker, and an honest person, but she didn't know how to relate to people. She came across as a person who was very conservative, a rule-watcher, a good time spoiler—the person who knows how late the hour is and is the first to say it's best to get on home.

In her late thirties, she hasn't married. She works in a technical profession in the television industry, but wants to get married and have a child. Two men have proposed to her, yet she has refused them as being too boring. Kari prefers to date wild men who will never marry, who are abusive to themselves and to herself. A psychologist might consider this "projection"— finding someone who is acting out the wild part of her personality that she can't express. Kari's relationships always start out with what I call the "fixer-upper theme." The men are talented men, down on their luck, they just need

Figure 14

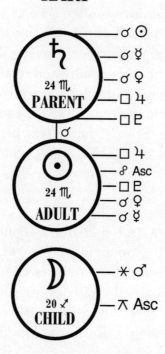

some parenting, someone to keep them from the booze, pot, card tables, whatever. Kari nurses them back to health and then they leave her, often with a terrible confrontation.

Kari loves the nursing and she loves the fight. The nursing proves she can be loving. The fight proves that her values are right, even though she loses the man. I tried to suggest that she was trying to be a mother surrogate and that the separation was what happens when boys decide to leave their mothers. Kari is a good worker; she had taken to going to a lot of what I call "hug workshops," or new age relationship work. Slowly she is starting to loosen up and gain a better insight to her overly structured personality. She is learning to allow herself to be herself. She is lucky.

For our toxic pattern work here, it is important to note that in Kari's Parent conjunct Adult, the ego spheres share the same aspects with the same planets: Jupiter, Mercury, Venus, and Pluto. The Parent's influence is working with the same planets as the Adult, making it doubly difficult for the Adult to gain the necessary distance, psychologically, to exercise its own individuality. Everything blurs as the Adult's options are dominated by the Parent's blurred boundaries. How can one grow up when what it means to be an adult is distorted?

Saturn conjunct Moon (figure 15) symbolizes the Parent energy contaminating that of the Child. With this configuration, the Parent refuses to understand the Child's emotional needs and imposes upon the Child the Parent's emotional expectations. Sometimes individuals with this problem act like little adults when they are children; they become rule-mongers who want everyone to obey. They tell on people in school for rule infractions. There is a bit of the bully in this profile. The Child/Parent can't stand seeing other children having fun, so an attack is launched, either by outright physical dominance, or with psychological dominance.

As adults, these individuals can be perceived as angry children who didn't get enough play time to discover who they were and what delighted them. Delight has no place in the Parent-dominated Child. Work is the main theme; another is rebellion. The Child may have a split personality, with one half a perfect little angel; the other, a vicious devil. The devil is the Child's angry statement about having a punishing Parent. These children are so angry that any authority becomes fair game for secret, if not open, assault.

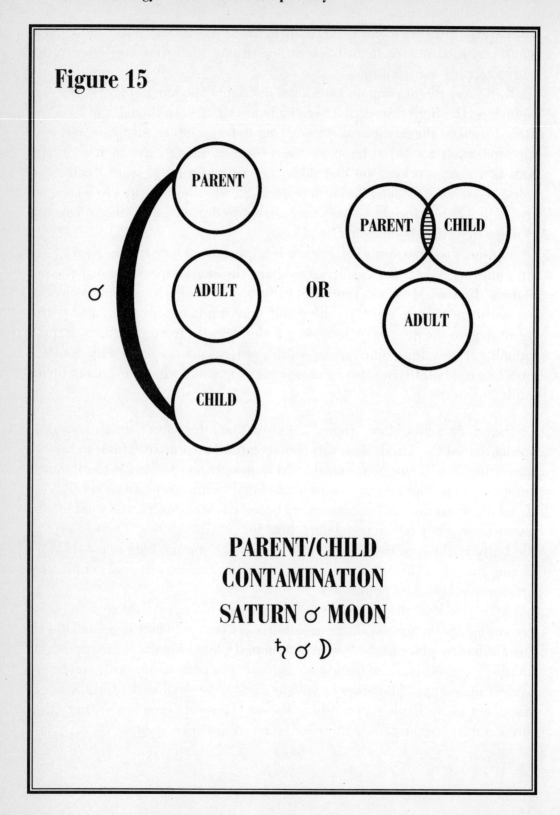

Figure 15

PARENT

ADULT

CHILD

♂

OR

PARENT CHILD

ADULT

**PARENT/CHILD
CONTAMINATION
SATURN ♂ MOON
♄ ♂ ☽**

Figure 16

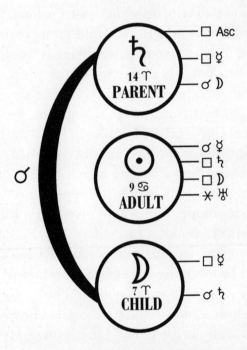

FRANK

**PARENT/CHILD
CONTAMINATION**

ħ ♂ ☽

Frank

Figure 16 is the chart of a man we will call Frank. Frank has the Parent/Child or Saturn/Moon conjunction. Frank was quite unstable. He was brilliant as a production manager, but the rest of his life was chaotic. He would get involved in wild activities that can only be described as those of a Child in rebellion. The Parent could not keep the Child repressed. At times the Child would come out in crazy ways. He would have orgies at his home. Then the Parent would assert its power and he would suddenly join a very expensive health gym, go on a special diet, buckle down, and get a lot of work done. But this good behavior wouldn't last for long. After a while his Child would want puerile sex, and Frank would go to Vegas and spend money on hookers. He loved it when one of his girlfriends would dress up like a dominatrix to excite him. What is the image of the whip and leather dominatrix but that of a dominating parent?

Frank loved power struggles. He thought he was good at winning. His drive was childlike. During the Olympics in Los Angeles he became competitive about Olympic pins, gaining a massive collection. He loved to make bets, to ogle women passing by, to bait the unions, and to "out-Cadillac" his competition. Frank was often with people but complained of feeling all alone. Perhaps he hoped that competition would give him a breakthrough and one of his wins would deliver him unto himself.

Frank had been married three times when he came to see me. He was not afraid of the altar; he loved the struggle to see who was really in control. Actually, he was really a large Bronx playground bully. In his session with me he tried to draw me into some competitive games. Just how good an astrologer was I? Who had I really helped? Did I think I was psychic or what? After an initial consultation, I referred Frank to a hypnotherapist who was able to reduce his regressive struggle between Inner Parent and Inner Child. He is now married for the fourth time, and, at this writing, the marriage is working.

The Adult/Child contamination is represented by the Sun/Moon conjunction (figure 17). This configuration is developmentally confusing, for the Adult imposes its energies onto the Child, often robbing something from the childhood. In theory, the Adult dominance of the Child is not as negative as that of the Parent/Child (Saturn conjunct Moon). However, making such a distinction is a close call. The Child is expected to perform to standards not of his or her own. There is the quality of the nerd to some of this, of the boring, bright child who doesn't know what it is like to be a child.

Figure 17

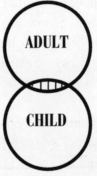

ADULT/CHILD
CONTAMINATION

People with an Adult/Child contamination may act like little professors. These people will seek to appear uninvolved, concerned only about facts, and happy to offer critical or objective opinions in a sometimes abrasive way.

For this archetype, dating is difficult. These people want everything to go according to a script. They will find spontaneous conversations, open expressions of feelings, and intuitive activities (governed by the Moon) hard to get into. At work these individuals are often the super employee, the yuppie who takes off like a rocket. Yet there are problems with authority, and problems with not being able to fraternize with peers and fellow employees.

Diana

Figure 18 is the astro-analysis chart of a woman we'll call Diana, the daughter of a prominent Los Angeles psychologist. Diana had been super-straight, an overachiever in high school and college. She'd gone to camp every summer as a child and performed well. She was independent. She had a problem—she knew very little about love. She knew how to get "positive reinforcement" by following her father's prodding (Saturn square Sun and Moon). She was always quite responsible but never seemed to have fun, just "satisfactory feedback" instead.

The reality of her plight came to a crisis point when her father divorced her mother to marry a patient who had been in therapy with him for 12 years. This fall from grace of the father also caused a suspicion of the rules he had taught her about fun and a fulfilling life. Also, she took "losing my father to another woman" hard and with great anger (Mars conjunct Sun and Moon). Her father broke his own rules by marrying a client. In her anger, she wondered if her father had been having sex with this woman in his consultation room.

Actually, Diana's rebellion produced a real psychological rebirth. The boring Diana faded out and a more real one took her place. While it was a struggle, her skills were such that she could cope. She saw me from time to time to work on her Inner Child notebooks. In these consultations I was able to witness her growth and share the thrill that she was experiencing as she worked through her new awakening. One of the great things about Tri-Astral analysis is seeing people grow, overcoming the challenges of circumstance to become strong enough to choose their destiny and their own path.

It was a dance class and experiencing the freedom of motion that finally led Diana to herself. Through dance she got in touch with her Inner Child. Also, she utilized the Mars and Uranian energy active in both spheres. As a physically mature person she had the insight to want to defend her Child, and

Figure 18

DIANA

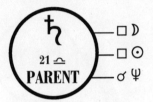

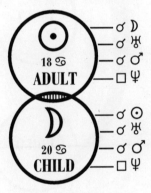

ADULT/CHILD
CONTAMINATION

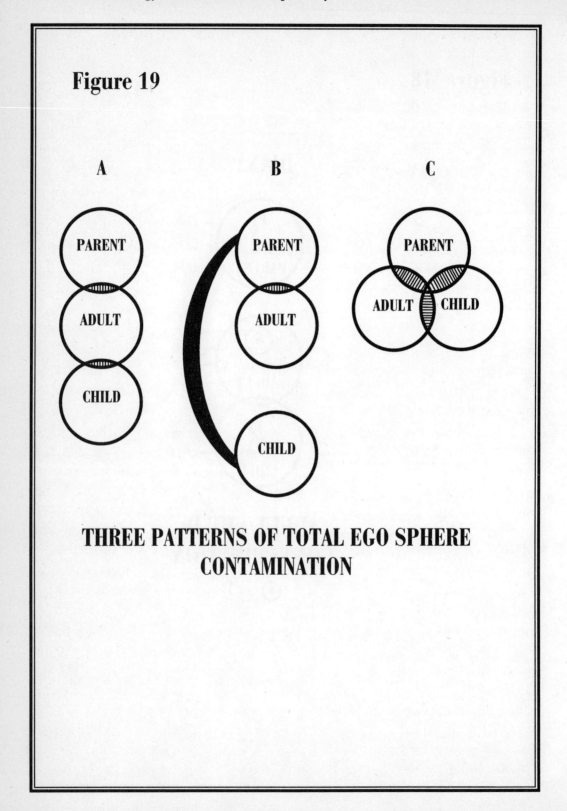

Figure 19

A   B   C

PARENT   PARENT   PARENT

ADULT   ADULT   ADULT   CHILD

CHILD   CHILD

**THREE PATTERNS OF TOTAL EGO SPHERE
CONTAMINATION**

by working with her whole body in motion she was able to start a playlike process which brought her to a happier, more spontaneous life.

The most restrictive and toxic configuration is when all three ego spheres are clustered together in a conjunction or stellium (figure 19 A, B, and C). Here the Parent has contaminated the Adult and Child. The self is a blur and there are no boundaries. Saturn rules the three ego spheres like a dictator. There is a sense of a controlling air about this individual. It is as if the Parent ego sphere is the thought police and has a stake-out monitoring the Adult and the Child.

The pervasive influence of the Parent restricts the emotional polarities and openness of the responses. For example, the swing of this type of personality can vary. On one hand there can be a strong drive to be efficient, to keep up high discipline, to perform with control, and to always keep the goals in mind. The place of play is reduced; the emphasis on achievement is high.

There is also the flip side which can manifest in the potential capacity for nearly fanatical obedience and loyalty to a person or a cause. This person can join extreme clubs or societies, or merely get overly zealous to please the boss. There is often a sadistic streak working here. The Parent ego sphere considers that nearly everyone has been raised "soft," therefore everyone should have to work hard. Look out if this psychological type is your supervisor or manager, for the driving whip is in the hands of a person who will use it. This anger is fueled by an on-going sense of desperation, a fear of not measuring up, of being jealous of other people who have made it because they had it easy or got the breaks.

Curiously, there can often be blind loyalty to abusive parents who are falsely seen as saints, but who are in reality not at all like the projected image the Child is carrying. The Child imagines that his or her parents were great; their upbringing was great; they were self-sacrificing. Upon investigation, a classic case of denial will often be seen at work here. The wish projection is that the parents were great; denial blocks the real facts. Excuses are made. Dad was a great dad—he was hard, tough, didn't raise any sissies and he would have gone farther if he had gotten the breaks. In truth, Dad was a fearsome drunk who bitched about work all the time and had low self-esteem which his child picked up on.

Usually the Adult ego sphere enables a person to maintain an independent sense of reality, of emotional balance. But in this pattern the Adult is also overwhelmed by the Parent's prejudices, disinclinations, and reality tests.

When fun is rejected, a perverse idea that work is fun develops. A stern, puritanical ethic is okay in certain circumstances. Work becomes a way to badger other people. Fun is making other people get to work. Obviously this has limitations—who has this Parent ever made happy?

Lilly

Figure 20 is that of Lilly. Lilly's father was a wild-catter in the oil fields of Texas. He was a hard drinker and lived a life of hard work. He was abusive; Lilly married at age 18 to get away from him. While her husband proved to be no better than her dad, at least she could divorce him, which she did. Lilly moved to California and got involved in the great expansion. She was tough, a hard worker; she became a real estate agent, married another agent, and they built a rich life with two kids and a great house.

Still, Lilly's psyche had a homing device that enabled her to find a man like Daddy, a man who would mistreat her. She divorced and remarried, and her second husband proved he could not handle affluence by drinking and running around. He claimed Lilly had nagged him to death; that she wanted his "balls." Divorce number two came along and Lilly hit the bottle. She worked herself ragged. Things hit bottom when she was arrested for drunk driving. She spent some time in jail and then joined Alcoholics Anonymous. After all this she decided to consult with an astrologer.

Lilly needed to overcome drinking and a negative self-image brought on by parental abuse. She was able to work with a journal for 18 months, keeping an emotional diary that enabled her to see the pattern of her thoughts for herself. Sober and more aware of her self-destructive urges, Lilly is back at work and is thinking about buying a restaurant.

It is important when one sees any of the contaminating formulas given in this chapter to take an especially close look at that particular chart and ego sphere formation. Toxic patterns such as these are powerful and can have a very pervasive effect. Consider it like a dye in water—once a dye is there, it affects everything in some manner. Like salt in coffee, even a little is too much.

This is not to suggest that all individuals with these configurations are doomed, like some tragic position in a chess problem where checkmate is forced. Rather, these are situations that are likely to be tricky. And by definition, if something is known to be difficult or complex, people will have greater problems handling it. Coping skills must be learned.

Figure 20

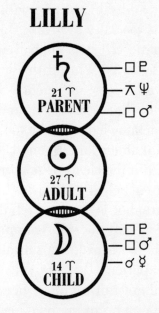

PARENT/ADULT/CHILD CONTAMINATION

♄ ☌ ☽

♄ ☌ ☉

The key here is to know when the astrologer should be frank about a toxic situation and when to be subtle. Knowing how to shape the communication of advice is as important as the advice itself. The metaphorical approach is one that gives an image which is relatively clear.

A way to show a person how toxic contamination works is to take a glass of water and gradually add salt, starting with a little and adding only a little more, until the water is too salty to drink. Don't explain exactly why you are doing this. The dramatic effect is such that the impact will be anchored deeply. And the final result is: What if this were the only water available for you to drink? Salty water does not quench a thirst, it creates a compulsive need for more water, but the water is contaminated.

When the water is acknowledged to be too salty, ask how the person would get the water to be drinkable again. Some will offer the idea of adding something to offset the salt. But the clear- or scientific-headed individuals will realize that the only way to get clear water is to boil it and condense the steam.

Once this basic metaphor is grasped, tell the person to imagine that his or her Parent ego sphere is like the salt, contaminating his or her psyche. The person's task is to reclaim his or her Adult and Child from this toxic spill. If the individual is to experience self-growth, at least in terms of Tri-Astral analysis, the individual must distill his or her true nature. To do this, the person must find a way to pull his or her own personality out of the Parental toxins that have contaminated it. This means personal work.

The first step to take here is mindfulness—to be mindful of your consciousness and what you are doing. You must be aware of your actions. Take the time to be an observing ego and watch yourself without being judgmental.

The second step is to keep a realistic journal of thoughts and actions. Seeing thoughts written down can in and of itself be therapeutic. Rereading a diary also gives one a chance to see patterns more objectively, to see where to set goals for change.

The third step is to understand that healing is a process of integrating old feelings with new positive affirmations about the future. Become aware of your bad habits. Give them names; personalize them. Now they can disappear like some of the bad friends you've already managed to exclude from your life.

The fourth step is to make personal audio or video tapes about your life, what you see yourself doing, and what you want to do. If it is an audio tape, listen to it in the car. Keep revising and updating the tapes, saving a few of them for review at a later time. This process of working with the recorded voice produces dramatic changes.

One of my clients beat a bad eating habit his mother had encouraged. He made a tape upon which he called his eating personality Mr. Clean Plate. He called his mother Mrs. Seconds. Mr. Clean Plate personified his mother's demand that he clean up his plate. Mrs. Seconds is the mother who was always putting more food on the plate—a sense of maternal nature gone out of control. The feeder, the nurturer, and the pusher were all rolled into one toxic parent.

Mr. Clean Plate, the compulsion to eat, died a metaphorical death. My client learned to push food away and refuse to eat more. He became mindful of his real appetite. This victory over food enabled my client to take a new attitude about himself. He was a winner.

My heartfelt philosophy is that anyone can be a winner. Work with an open heart and a will to be the best you can be and there will always be results, there will always be change. Not as fast as is sometimes desired, but if the will is strong the changes will accrue. Motivation is very important, as is a clear metaphor for the problem. With this basis in solid insight, the results will be rewarding. Always be aware of your mistakes and keep learning how to improve. You will discover that your positive personal habits will create a healing process for the psyche to grow and mend.

Figure 21

ROBERTA

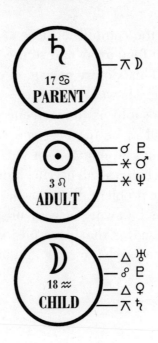

Chapter Four

Three balls the juggler throws up—
a basketball, a football, a tennis ball.
First they rotate wildly in the air,
now he dribbles them off the floor
and plays each one perfectly—
he knows how differently each will bounce.

★ ★ ☆ ★ ★ ☆ ★ ★

Pinball Wizard: Seeing How the Personality Bounces

She's Got Personality, Walk, Personality, Talk...

No two people are exactly the same. This is an important principle to understand when dealing with astrological and psychological energies. People are different and respond in varying degrees to what might appear to be the same stimulus.

The best example of this is to consider sunlight. The sun is the center of our solar system and its reflected light illuminates the planets. Take one hundred nude people, put them out in the sun for a couple of hours, and the different skin responses will be overwhelming. Some of the nudists will be burned to a crisp, some will be bright red, some will even be tan; others will seem to be unaffected, neither tan nor burned.

This example of the affect of the sun's rays on the nudists points out that while the exposure to the sun was a constant—a couple of hours—the results varied from individual to individual. The same principle is true with astrological or psychological energy. The issue is one of "relative effect," or different responses for different folks.

Another example is the fact that everyone responds differently to medicine and requires different dosages. Again, we are all unique in our response to a stimulus. This translates in astrology to an explanation of why people having the same planetary aspects, be it square or trine, will respond in ways distinctively their own.

The key to all these illustrations is that it is important to perceive the reaction level, or resonance of an individual. Resonance is a way of measuring the way a person responds to stimulus. In the nudist example we measured a type of resonance to the sun's rays. Those nudists who were sunburned had a high resonance; those who showed little effect had a low sun/skin resonance. There are several types of resonance to consider: emotional, mental, social, intellectual, physical. A person with high resonance has a quick, overly sensitive response to certain situations. Take stress—high resonance means stress gets to you quickly. Low resonance means that you can tolerate a lot.

Astrological resonance is a factor that is derived for each individual by an objective analysis of the perceived sensitivity of an individual based upon the weight of their aspects. The key is the personal history. For example, the psychological tension of a Saturn square is more apparent in some people than in others. The skilled practitioner of Tri-Astral analysis not only must understand the relative weight (i.e., the number and types of aspects) of the ego spheres, but the biographical data as well. You must determine how strongly the individual has been responding to the astrological configurations. To understand this requires a review of character and personal history. For one individual a strong Saturn is a crushing blow from authority; to another, it is a stimulus to achieve. The difference, of course, could be in other planetary pictures that need to be understood. But on the whole it is important to determine how sensitive the client's past reactions to different stimuli seems to be. From this you derive their level of resonance. Remember, the higher the level of resonance, the more sensitive the individual.

In Chapter 2 we demonstrated the method by which astrologically weighted ego spheres could be created so that astro-analysis could begin the process of giving insight into the driving forces of that particular aspect of the personality. The key is quite simply to look for the most heavily aspected ego sphere, the most "weighted." This is the dominant ego sphere whose aspect total makes it the most energy-charged. This sphere of consciousness, as it were, is the hub of the most numerous and complete psyche energy interactions. As in music, this dominant sphere is the dominant chord or harmonic schemata, and its themes will affect the other two spheres. Its resonance is most important, for it is the pulse—the bass line, as it were—for the basic psychological rhythms of the personality.

John Lennon

In John Lennon's astro-analysis chart (figure 12), the Child is the dominant ego sphere and it will color the games of John's life. By games we mean those cognitive patterns formed by personal energy transactions, meaning John's exchanges with other people. John's Child sphere has the greatest aspect weight and if the Child gets too many negative "residuals," he will regress to an infantile tantrum.

A residual is a repressed fragment of an energy charge that resides within the ego sphere after an interaction. It can build up energy in a number of ways. It may build up like static electricity from internal friction. It can be a product of personality games which are not venting energy properly. The pay-off is usually a blow-up, a release of steam or residual energy. One of the games the Child sphere plays is "Parents don't know anything!" The game works this way. The Child sphere in one individual hooks the Parent sphere of another person to a problem—the meaning of love, the nature of life, why the good die young. In the interactions working with this issue, a residual negative charge is built up as the Child is told answers that don't satisfy it. After all, who can really answer such questions? The residuals mount up until the Child, in a fit of rage, rejects all these answers and screams, "What do you know, I'll have to do this myself!"

The Child, the rebel, is important in John Lennon's chart and in his life. A spokesman against authority, the war in Vietnam, the older generation, the tyranny of the old ways of thinking—these are the dominant issues of Lennon, and all are reflected in his Child ego sphere. Play, spontaneous creativity, and the new are what he elevates.

Roberta

Let's look at the chart (figure 21) of Roberta, a client I had who played this anti-authority game through her dominant Child. Roberta's Child sphere is the most weighted, and this sphere is connected to the Adult by Pluto. Roberta was the wife of a motion picture studio head. She manifested an activation in that her highly resonant Child sphere went about asking the meaning of life. Her studio head husband had no interest in this; he had movies to make. He gave her cash and told her to go shopping. She found herself interested in a guru her husband hated. She started attending this guru's study classes.

Rightly or wrongly, the guru told Roberta that he was praying for her and her husband's success.

As it happened, Roberta's husband had a huge hit, a blockbuster. The guru asked for a contribution, since he had prayed so hard for that movie to make it. Roberta asked her husband what he thought of making a contribution and the reply was to forget the whole thing.

Let's review what has been going on. Roberta has been playing a game from the Child sphere. The game is, "Who can teach me?" The guru is playing along with the game by saying, "I'll play and pray for you, which is my game." Her husband is playing the bad guy who doesn't want to play into any of this; his game is that anyone can see the power of money. Roberta's emotional residuals (negative pay-offs) with her husband build up, and the discharge comes when Roberta gives the guru a check for $750,000. This relieves the power struggle of Pluto opposite her Moon. Roberta's Child does the deed, facing the monster.

Roberta's husband hits the roof, as anyone might imagine, but it is too late—not only has the guru cashed the check, he has skipped town. And although the husband did track the guru down and personally pummel him, the money could not be recovered. Roberta's Child won a round. And the guru, by successfully playing her game, won some bucks.

The fallout was a divorce for Roberta. This is not surprising, for the stakes of the game were high. Roberta gave big bucks. Her husband, to my thinking, could have forgiven Roberta if she had slept with the guru, but money was his sacred area and she had violated that space. While this game may be a little extreme for most of us, it is a true story and the consequences are real. This is an example of a Child's game played with a big checkbook, which is what makes it memorable. In fact, when Roberta came in for a reading it was this incident that she told me early into the reading, recounting it with some childish pride. "See what I did to Daddy!" she seemed to be saying.

It is now apparent that a number of evaluations of ego spheres are necessary to understand a Tri-Astral chart. The first is to identify the three spheres as the dominant, subdominant, and third. The second is to evaluate whether the predominant emotional charge of each ego sphere is positive or negative.

Figure 22

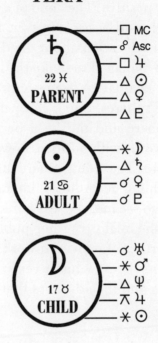

TERA

Tera

Tera (figure 22) is an interesting study. Notice that all three ego spheres are very active, with the dominant sphere being the Parent. It has the most "hits." The Child is the subdominant sphere, and the Adult is the third. What is immediately interesting about Tera's chart is that all the spheres are very active and all appear positive. The child of a successful businessman, Tera has lived a life of wealth and ease. However, she developed diabetes and has worked very hard for education about the disease. A divorce did create some cloudy skies, but she managed to make the best of the situation.

The key point in evaluating Tera's approach to life is to see the positive elements in all three spheres. She is not perfect, but she manages to have a dominant Parent sphere and not be a person that is overbearing. This is because her Saturn works with positive, flowing energy, thanks to trines to the Sun, Venus, and Pluto. The Adult sphere makes a trine to Saturn and a sextile to the Moon, enabling her Adult to interact and be the hub of her growth.

When Tera came to see me, she was bored. I suggested that since her Child is conjunct Uranus, she might try some public access television work for diabetes (Uranus is the ruler of television work). Tera accepted that advice with great enthusiasm, and she now has a very well-received show educating the public about diabetes and the advances that are being made in its treatment.

Mark

Mark (figure 23) is an example of the Adult sphere being the dominant consciousness with the Parent the subdominant. Mark is a successful media person in Los Angeles, a former anchorman of the evening news. He is very controlled and logical, very savvy of the politics of situations.

Mark might be considered too serious. He is always conscious of how he looks, never venturing out without wearing the perfect suit or sweater. His voice is very cultured and strong, as you would expect from someone who has spent a lifetime in radio and television.

What is most impressive, however, is Mark's ability to cope. At the height of his television career, he was fired in an overnight station management coup. He went from being big man on the town, always recognized by the public, to a man with no camera on him. His marriage fell apart. Life had given him a difficult blow.

It was the inventive Adult (Sun conjunct Uranus and Mercury) which helped Mark to find himself through forming his own production company. He struggled at first, doing coverage of local parades, business events, and

Figure 23

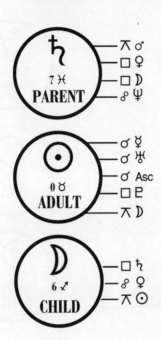

Figure 24

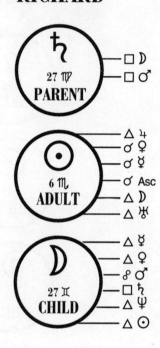

RICHARD

sporting events like soccer and tennis. His business grew. He kept a positive attitude and worked hard. I remember we had lunch in Hollywood one day when he told me proudly he was making twice as much with his own company as he did at the network.

Note also that the Child is Mark's weakest sphere. Mark doesn't manifest his Child well. He is all business. Moon square Saturn makes for a Child who feels judged, struggling for parental approval, and Mark was always perfectly put together. He kept his flaws covered, and it was difficult for him to open up and vent his anger.

What is most rewarding about Mark is his charity. He would give advice and encouragement to people, pointing them in directions where they might find assistance. He would call them to tell them of something that he had learned that might be helpful to them. Mark is now remarried and he was able to turn his life around.

Richard

The strong Adult is not always a sign of good, logical actions. Richard (figure 24) shows a Tri-Astral chart in which the resentful Parent is really calling the shots. The Saturn square Moon and Mars opposition Moon make this Child configuration very powerful. While the Adult has nice aspects, the Moon's square to the Parent/Saturn and opposition to Mars makes for a very mean little Child indeed. Through the Moon trine, the Child is able to poison the Adult. How can a trine lead to a toxic situation? This Adult sphere with that Moon trine is like having a direct phone line to an angry and vengeful person who hates his or her Parent and wants to call you 24 hours a day. The situation is restless; the Saturn has no other outlets except the hard aspects to the Moon and Mars, and this makes the lunar energies charged with anger.

But what about the trines? Some will ask if the trine will not make it better—smooth it out, so to speak. The astrologer Barbara Watters wrote extensively about crime and found that sometimes trines make one want to do things "the easy way." For Richard, the easy way was the way of a con artist. His Adult personality is a smooth front, a happy face through which a disturbed and angry Child strikes out. The Parent's squares to Moon and Mars is a T-cross in traditional astrology with Saturn at the finger, a difficult configuration.

On one level, Richard came to me to see if his business was "okay," and on another level he wanted to talk about his sex drive. He was running a variety of what we in Los Angeles call "scams," or questionable businesses. Richard was managing a questionable nursing home as well as dealing a little drugs and a little prostitution. When meeting him it was the last thing one would have guessed. Wearing nice designer clothes and driving a BMW, Richard seemed like a yuppie who was trying a new experience by seeing an astrologer.

The truth of the matter was that Richard was knee-deep in problems. A minor one was drugs, a major one was sex. Richard loved his cocaine (Neptune trines can often offer escape; in this case, that of his Child), which would eventually put him in jail. Also, Richard loved perverted sex. Saturn square Mars and Mars opposite the Moon made him enjoy tying people up and flagellating them. With the right woman, he would allow himself to be tied up. He told a very strange story about learning his lesson about bondage bars, which are bars where the bondage crowd can shop for fun. A woman had taken him home and handcuffed him to a bed for two days. He had to break the bed to escape. At least that was his story.

Like many people, Richard had a private myth that kept him going. He believed that he was blessed with a "sexual turbo-drive" and wanted to know if there was anything in his chart that would indicate this "fate." He would take it as a sign of luck. I approached Richard with caution. I told him that his problem stemmed from his childhood, where, in my opinion, he was either abused by a parent or by the neighborhood environment. He admitted to having a very "strong father" who wasn't afraid to "kick ass," but Richard could not confront this paternal figure. He just wanted to know if it was in his chart that he was oversexed, and therefore he could breathe a sigh of relief and claim that he couldn't help it if "sexual power" was his destiny.

I did not let him off easily. Realizing that Richard was looking for some validation, I strongly suggested that he seek counseling. "I can handle my sexuality," he said in his Scorpio way. "I just want to know if this is a cosmic condition; you know, ordained by the stars." The con artist in Richard had a field day with me. I was sincere and tried to be helpful, but the con artist in Richard just wanted to tell some stories and use this astrologer for his own validation processes.

Richard astonished me with wild tales of adventures in all kinds of sexual and business environments. He even tipped me for the reading, flashing a big wad of bills and giving me some extra cash for "vigorish," a gambling term meaning to raise the odds on the bet. I felt like a waiter delivering a table with a view. Later, I heard a rumor that Richard had gotten busted for fraud for violations in the management of his rest home. I wasn't surprised, for I wouldn't have purchased a used car from him. We are lucky, in a way—Richard could have gone into politics.

Eric

Figure 25 shows the Tri-Astral analysis chart of a young television executive we'll call Eric. Eric's chart is very balanced; the Child and Parent spheres are nearly the same planetary weight. The Moon has a slight edge in power because it conjuncts the ascendent. The key to understanding Eric is to see the Saturn trines to both Sun and Moon, allowing the Child and the Adult easy access to the Parent. With Saturn trining the Uranus conjunct the Sun, it is a very creative and quite innovative Parent.

Eric is a whiz kid. He has put together a small programming empire by the age of 37 that would make most older executives proud. He is a restless young man, not happy with his success and pushing for more. He radiates a very real energy, and a charismatic atmosphere that infects his young staff with the desire to please him and work long hours.

In the business ruled by Uranus (television and radio), Eric is a genius. His Uranus (trine Saturn, conjunct Sun) is superbly placed for knowing how to originate new ideas and develop them.

Eric's weak spot, and he has few in business, is in his private life. He has no private life. He works around the clock and has more frequent flier miles than Ted Turner. The inconjunct of Venus to Saturn shows Eric's difficulty with personal relationships. The square of Venus to the Moon means that his Inner Child is not comfortable with Venusian issues of playing house or vulnerable intimacy.

Eric likes women on his arm, on the television screen, and in the office. But he does not have the time to really develop a one-on-one relationship. He likes what I call "instant women," a lot like instant coffee. Just call up a starlet and have an instant date. This is not to say that Eric has sex with all these "instant women." Their purpose is to complete an evening; to generate an effect. Sleeping with these women would give them power over him, or suck up some of his energy—something Eric eschews with great wisdom. It is no wonder that his one marriage ended with his wife bailing out for a man who had less money, but more time to devote to her. Eric doesn't care, his love is his business and he is climbing fast. He will have his own jet in a year.

Sally

What a difference a planet makes! Figure 26 shows us Sally, who has Neptune conjunct the Sun or Parent. Sally is what I call a boom/buster. She has a boom of success and makes a lot of money, then loses it, goes bust or out of business, lies fallow for a while, and "booms" back into success only to bust again.

Figure 25

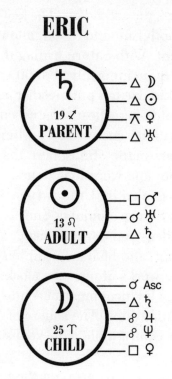

Figure 26

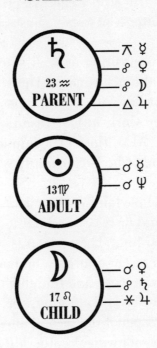

Notice that Sally has none of the flowing Parent/Saturn trines of Eric (figure 25). To my interpretation, the trine from Saturn to Jupiter is the key to her success. Neptune conjunct the Sun/Adult is the cause of the rise and fall of her success cycle. The Neptune gives her certain powers to project, to act out roles, and to be imaginative, but it is too close to the Adult sphere, too close to the Sun. This Neptune also erodes success, erodes the ego strength, or causes her determination to falter—or worse, causes her to misjudge or misperceive a situation.

The Saturn/Moon opposition as well as opposition to Venus keeps her Inner Child confused about intimacy. There is a need for distance for her Inner Child. Her Parent has wide boundaries. The result is a private childish life that is played after work in love affairs, several marriages, and other love-related problems. Also, the Sun conjunct Neptune rules the Moon in Leo, making for an adult who is constantly seeking some fogged memory of childhood.

Sally supports her whole family—her mom, dad, and her kids—plus meets often with an ex-husband or two. She went to an inexperienced but inexpensive shrink and seduced him. The woman is on the move. Her last business has gone bust, her mom has had surgery, and now Sally is in the seminar business teaching others how to cope and find themselves. Having built large businesses in two areas, jewelry and clothing, she is credible as a success on one level. She teaches the gospel of the second and third chance at life, at finding meaning and value. Her following is gathering and she wants to take her message on the road. Look out; Sally may be in your town next.

Joe

Joe (figure 27) is another example of why Neptune aspects need special consideration. Joe committed suicide. When an astrologer has a client shoot himself in the head, there is a strong sense of wondering how could this have happened, why couldn't it have been foreseen. Suicides can't easily be predicted, but the elements of escape were always in Joe's chart. The strong Neptune (trine Saturn and conjunct Sun) made him a dreamer, a traveler to distant lands. Joe had terrific collections of African art, all purchased in Africa. He was also an old-fashioned "pot-head," a man who smoked a little "tea" from time to time and made it a near-religious experience.

Note the Uranus conjunct the Parent. Saturn and Uranus are neurotic together, especially a 28° Taurus Saturn which is fixed, stubborn earth and a 0° Gemini Uranus which is mutable air. Joe was a little accident prone; he'd

Figure 27

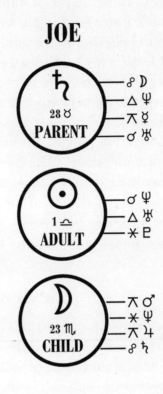

stumble on his own feet. His Parent was erratic; he worked at a steady job, but was a wanderer. His Adult was full of wild, romantic thoughts. The Neptune conjunction made him a dreamer. He saw things in his own way. During a career crisis he simply developed a love for the unknown release of death, and in a moment of dark fantasy shot himself.

Joe's access to his Inner Child was weak—the Mars and Jupiter inconjuncts spell trouble in believing in the adult world. Add to this Saturn opposing the Moon and here is a Child that cannot play except in the final and cosmic terms of a cruel Saturn/Parent. Joe, in an hour of crisis over his job (a parts man at an airplane plant), which was being terminated, took a gun to his head and said hello to eternity.

I cried when I heard. I'm passing this on here so that all can see that death can steal in through many doors. The power of the outer planets of Uranus Neptune, and Pluto are never to be underestimated, especially in square and conjunction. Neptune touched each of the ego spheres in Joe's chart, and he shot himself during a fit of hopelessness. The illusion of death become more than life, it became a romantic embrace with the great beyond.

Review

Let's review what we have learned in this chapter. The rule is to understand that each of the ego spheres responds differently to one another and to outside stimulation due to its sign and to its planetary aspects. In the majority of the cases, the most aspected ego sphere is called the dominant. The second most aspected sphere is the subdominant, and the least aspected is called the third.

The interaction between these three weighted ego spheres is a three-way dynamic, a weaving of these points of consciousness. One of the most interesting facets of this astro-analysis approach is that the most active personality trait may not represent the strongest sphere. If someone has a Parent for a dominant and a Child as the subdominant spheres, the Child may appear most active, but that is because it is acting out of rebellion. Hopefully with work and insight the Adult may be taught to bring reason and growth to such a situation.

This chapter began with a poem about the importance of knowing how differently balls of varying shape bounce in the juggler's toss. Using astro-analysis it is possible to learn about yourself. How do the different parts of your consciousness "bounce"? What is your dominant sphere, subdominant, and third? How does their relationship work for you? When one observes oneself for a while and starts to see the dynamics of the energy transfers in his or her own personality, it become easier to see it functioning in other people.

The key is to start observing the different energies of those you know or with whom you work. Learn to construct the Tri-Astral charts. Start a book of Tri-Astral charts and patterns. A simple three ring-binder or a series of file folders is all you need to begin. Take the time to record the chart and basic aspect analysis of dominant, subdominant, and third. Take notes on your subjects from time to time. As you progress and start reflecting on someone and this system of looking at their personal energies, you will find that you get a tighter and tighter focus on them and the inner games of love and life that they play.

As you continue this discipline, you will find that you start changing. You become more careful in how you approach people; you start making changes in your own habits because by knowing your own chart you can now see yourself and others in a new dimension. This self-help tool works in the same way a mirror does, reflecting the true dimensions. Tri-Astral analysis is a reflection of the psycho-dynamics of the three faces of the self. When you use this powerful mirror you get directly to the heart of the matter. At this deep psychological level perception and change work together as one hand washes the other. You can't change a negative trait until you perceive it.

Observe the ways aspects work in affecting the ego spheres and you will be able to scan the psychology of most individuals. Such insight gives you an edge, a depth of understanding. Remember, discipline is the mother of insight when using this system. Work with the system and you will reap the rewards of learning to be a master player in the game of life.

Figure 28

RENNI

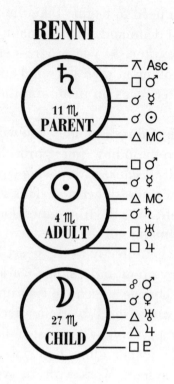

Chapter Five

See the Magician reach into his pocket
pulling out ball after ball with a grin.
A lady from the audience is asked to assist!
The Magician shows nothing up his sleeve
before pulling two big balls from her blouse
while the audience howls for more.

★ ★ ☆ ★ ★ ☆ ★ ★

Handicapping the Sexual Games

Yes, I'm the Great Pretender

When you think about it, sexuality is akin to athletics. It is a physical, biological activity and, while it can be practiced alone, most often it is a form of one-on-one wrestling, or dance. As one pop tune puts it, let's get "body to body!" On some rare occasions, usually bacchanalian events, sex can be a group sport. This is certainly not everyone's cup of tea. Most people see a distinct difference between sex and love. Sex can be an expression of love, but sex often occurs without love. It has its own appetite, like that one has for eating, drinking, sky-diving, or ballroom dancing. It can be performed with a separate gusto, a thrill of intensity different from deep amorous feelings.

As a physical act, sex is an expression of biological urges, carnal compatibility, and the need for corporeal release. As students of Tri-Astral analysis, our question is, "Which ego sphere is most connected to the sensations of the body?" My answer: the Child, or the Moon ego sphere, is the key. The Child is the most open we'll ever be, the body electric, the physical instincts, and the reflexes. The Child exploring his or her body is a handy metaphor for the way we come to feel and explore our sexuality.

Remember, we are not talking about love and the give-and-take of caring. Love and its many components (such as commitment and sharing) will be discussed fully in the next chapter. At issue here is the way that people express their sexual natures. Can they enjoy sex? Can they be playful with foreplay or copulation, or is sex seen as some guilt-ridden function? Often people are single or divorced because of sexual problems that became compounded through interaction. Sex is a turnstile that we have all passed through in this life. It was a rite of passage for some that never stopped. For others it is a confusing gate, to say the least.

"As the twig is bent, so grows the tree"—this adage has particular poignancy for the Child ego sphere. For truly as the Child is nurtured, so grows the Adult. If the Child has love and open expression, he or she sprouts up strong and open. If the child is abused and subjected to extreme punishment, either corporal or spiritual, the Child's expression of sexuality will reflect that.

One example from this author's personal experience will illustrate this point. For a while in my apprentice years I was a writer/stringer for a New York-based magazine that specialized in sexual subjects. The editor called and wanted me to go to a "spanking" massage parlor and see what was going on. My report would contribute some notes to a larger article they were compiling on the broad subject of "whatever gets you off," a spicy look at sexual relief.

At the spanking massage parlor it was surprising to learn that the management had a peep hole through which one could watch people be spanked until they had an orgasm. They gave me a free peep, since I was a journalist, but they regularly sold "dungeon viewing rights" to voyeurs who would also have a sexual experience just watching.

These individuals hiring their own spankings were not sleazy people with rude appearances, but well-dressed professional people. As children they had been abused at home or at school in such a way that they could reach orgasm through vigorous spanking. When the pop singer Madonna sang "spanky, spanky," she knew the vast numbers of abused Child ego states that would resonate to the message of that song. As the Child is bent, so grows the Adult.

In a real way, every ego sphere has something to do with sexuality. If Mars is conjunct or square the Parent/Saturn, the chances are good that this person will have a real performance conflict in many aspects of life, including sexuality. The Parent/Saturn is always measuring, always testing Mars. It is for this reason that the Parent ego sphere is second to the Child in importance in understanding sexual matters.

Renni

Consider the Tri-Astral diagram (figure 28) of Renni (again, not her real name). The trained eye sees immediately the contamination of the Parent and Adult ego spheres (Saturn conjunct Sun). Look at the heavy conjunctions the Parent and Adult are carrying, not to mention the square to Mars and inconjunct to the ascendant.

Renni's heavy Parent and Adult manifested as a woman who knew tons of rules about the natural laws of life. She was a body worker and could manipulate the body in ways that rivaled those used by a chiropractor. She was short and cute, with a quick smile. She never ate meat, stuck to a strict policy of no smoking in her presence, read good books, and listened to new age or classical music.

However, Renni had one vice—sex. Her Child has healthy trines; the Moon trine Uranus comes quickly to the eye as helping her be experimental and free, the Moon trine Jupiter shows a willingness to get totally involved, and the square to Pluto shows a dark and transforming sexuality and sex appeal. The Moon/Child opposition Mars along with the squared Pluto (the ruler of her Adult in Scorpio) gives her even more sexual attraction as well as a steaming, hot quality. People look at her when she walks into a room—there is something about her. This Mars opposition and Pluto square also give her a strong temper, as well. She could really erupt when she got mad. She was bullying people about smoking long before it was a national issue. She needed this anger to protect her because Renni often got into strange situations when she went about her massage work.

Prior to the advent of AIDS there was a lot more casual sex than is freely practiced today. In the late 1970s, Renni fit right in to this loose, experimental approach to sex. She was a party girl. She lost her virginity at age 15, slipping out her bedroom window and running wild. She liked sex, the way it felt, and she liked being popular. After completing her massage training, she entered into the Hollywood community and found that by sleeping with her customers she got huge tips and great referrals. To this day she knows the sexual habits of an astounding number of celebrities. But they couldn't smoke when she was around them, and she remains a vegetarian.

To Renni, there is a big difference between getting big tips for massages that sometimes end in sex than for directly charging a price for the sexual act.

It was during this period that Renni also experimented with lesbian lovers, because "women give better oral sex than men." Finally, after several years of all this, she met a young lawyer and settled down to an old-fashioned monogamous relationship. They haven't gotten married, but they have a living arrangement. Renni has gone back to school; she wants to be a writer. Certainly we would all like to read her memoirs.

Renni did this astrologer the good favor of sending some of her friends in for readings. A couple of her male friends said Renni was a "sex goddess;" that she knew all this body worker magic and became Aphrodite in bed.

What enabled Renni to stop this behavior was the growing AIDS threat and her own strong will. When she plugs that powerful Parent sphere into a project, her will is like iron. At this writing, she is still living happily with her lover.

Many of us have heard the expression "sexual athlete" in reference to someone who has great sexual prowess. And in the study of athletes the Child or the Moon is very important in assessing the success of an individual. One of the best resources in this endeavor is the *Gauquelin Book of Charts* which has many charts of athletes.

Pete Rose

Pete Rose illustrates this principle of the Moon and sexual and athletic prowess quite well. Figure 29 show Rose's Tri-Astral analysis chart. The Parent sphere is interested in fame (trine midheaven). Rules were made for the other guy (Saturn conjunct Jupiter), and don't get me mad (Saturn square Mars).

The Adult sphere is difficult. The two inconjuncts, especially the Sun to the Moon, indicate a reluctance to grow up. And Rose made a living playing a boy's game for big bucks.

It is the Child sphere of Rose's chart that spells out his personality. The opposition to Uranus makes for a shifting mentality, one looking for new games and new thrills like gambling. The trines to Pluto and Mercury make him coordinated and sexy. Rose was a legend not only with the bat but with the groupies that follow the big-league baseball players around. In person he radiates a strong masculine energy; his eyes are rangy, always looking about the room.

The ruler of the Child sphere in Sagittarius is Jupiter, which is conjunct Saturn (Parent) and trine the midheaven (MC). The Moon receives great

Figure 29

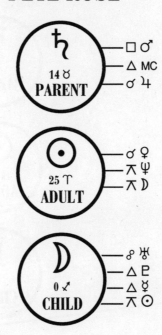

PETE ROSE

Figure 30

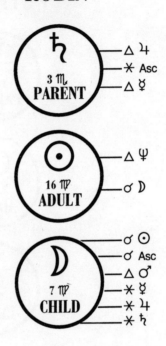

energy, a winning drive, and a will to break records and rules from this con-figuration. Rose is as happy as a child in the garden of sensual delights; he is delighted with the sexual smorgasbord that accompanies being the hit king and Mr. Hustle of the Big Leagues. The big salaries the Child/Athlete can generate now makes us much more aware of their private lives.

Remember, the issue in this discussion is whether the individual is good at sex, whether he or she is able to perform the act in good form and with enjoy-ment. Certain individuals with high traditional ethical standards attached to sex may not be able to conceive of relationships where good sex is not accom-panied by love and concern, where the common denominator is the first chakra. Astrologers who have had a wide public practice will know that such sex for its own sake does go on, despite the lack of other interests in the rela-tionship. In Los Angeles, a radio talk show host had a program devoted to callers who had seduced the pizza man or had sex in an unusual location with someone they hardly knew. His lines were jammed. Some people were evi-dently getting more than pizzas delivered.

Let's review one of the key issues in understanding the sexuality of an indi-vidual: understand the sign and element of the client's Moon. The sign and element of the Moon give the essential sexual sensibility; the aspects often give hints about initiation to the sex act or tastes in sexual conduct.

Robin

Robin (figure 30) has a Moon in Virgo. This is an earthy Moon which tends to respond in a slower fashion to the passions of romance. Being a Virgo Moon means that there is an analytical distance, especially at the beginning of things, toward a lover. The flaws and idiosyncrasies are noted, and romance takes time to manifest. There is undoubted a "pickiness" to the emotional Child. Robin seems to be a very happy, sexually well-adjusted person. Her Child sphere has a flowing trine to Mars as well as stimulating sextiles to Sat-urn, Jupiter, and Mercury. The conjunction to the ascendant by the Moon makes her a nurturer.

Robin came for a reading which had nothing to do with her sex life. Actu-ally her sex life has gone along well, which is why her chart is being examined. She has been in a steady relationship for some time and has a history of at least four year-long relationships (a long time, by Los Angeles standards). She was initiated into sexual intercourse by her college boyfriend with whom she

Figure 31

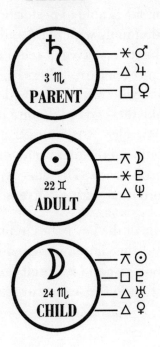

had a long relationship. All the "soft" aspects to the Moon would tend to indicate that her sexual experience was a normal flowering, not a violent, shocking violation by some testosterone nightmare.

The problem for Robin is the absence of squares pushing any of her ego spheres. She lacked ambition and was stuck in an entry-level job at a television station. She seemed content to go with the flow until one day she awoke to discover she was 35 years old and still in that entry-level position.

One of things about a happy life is that it may not be a life of high achievement and ambition. Content with a good relationship, a good sex life, and a job she knew well and which paid her half of the bills, Robin just floated. When she realized that she was drifting she did put out some effort. She consulted this astrologer, studied through some university extension programs, gained a new focus on herself, and now has been promoted to a managerial job, which is challenging her to use more of her diplomatic potential. She is an example of excellent growth and balance, even though she still has no plans for marriage.

Terry

In contrast, Terry's Tri-Astral chart (figure 31) is similar to Robin's, but with one exception—the square of Pluto to the Moon. Pluto squares motivate, but can also make one vulnerable to excess. The god Pluto was the rapist of Penelope. With his helmet that made him invisible he was the Lord of the Underworld. Terry was not exactly raped, but she was introduced to sexuality in a rough way by a drunken boyfriend while still in high school.

Terry became a body conditioning expert. She taught aerobic exercise classes, and slept around for some time with lots of partners even while living with an older man who had a vasectomy. The man had children from a previous marriage and had "closed the baby shop." Terry and this man would fight loudly over getting his vasectomy reversed so they could have kids. Terry hung on for three years before bailing out to be with a man closer to her age. She got married and presently has a baby girl.

From her descriptions of her sexual adventures, Terry approached sex like an gym workout. There were lots of different positions to be done and a certain amount of time had to be spent and a certain amount of sweat generated if it was to be considered a success.

Terry's Moon is in Scorpio, a fixed water sign, squared by its own ruler. It is interesting to note that the Moon also inconjuncts the sun which sextiles Pluto. This configuration is a minor learning triangle, and in Terry's case shows that she is capable of learning quickly and moving on. As a marketing person she represented different products, from printing to health foods, and did quite well in a tough market. She did not "float" as Robin did, and it is certainly plausible to look to Terry's Pluto square as one of the definite motivations for ambition as well as a signal of deep sexual desires and the edge to pursue them.

Liz

Liz represents the Moon in Aries (figure 32) with a square from Uranus. Liz is full of motivation. She is a power-seeker; a broker. In the world of television game shows she is the one who determines who will go on the show. While the producers are supposed to have the final say, Liz's independent Parent/Saturn soon makes sure that the producer's approval of contestants is only a formality. She decides. She is the power. The wide but operative Mars conjunct Saturn makes her a performance fanatic; she pushes herself hard to do well and roots for every contestant that she gets on that television game show stage. They are her actors, her stage children.

Sexually, Liz is in a realm that most men dream about. She is a super performer. She has sexy clothes and sexy underwear, and when they are all off, she is a sexy gal who likes sex like a good steak—and she knows just how to season it. The queen of Club Med, the toast of Beverly Hills, she was wildly promiscuous only between boyfriends. Finding one who can "deliver the pizza" for the enormous sexual appetite she is packing is a problem. She went through doctors, lawyers, and directors. She "wasted" four years of her life with a writer in a relationship that was just sex for its own sake. Jilted, she turned to a year-long affair with a well-known though married celebrity. The sex was "great," but she tired of being the "other woman" and finally left that arrangement. At last word she was living with another writer, hoping for a secure relationship.

Liz remains one of my favorite clients. Mars trine Sun and Moon square Uranus makes for a lively individual who is full of energy and can see the comic side of life. Being something of a comedian, she amused this astrologer with a story about her reaction to an encounter with her first uncircumcised man. "There's a whole other universe out there," she quipped.

Vicky

In many ways Vicky (figure 33) was a very difficult client. At first glance the most obvious problem is the contaminated Parent and Child ego spheres, symbolized by the Saturn/Sun conjunction. The problem is further exacerbated by the unaspected Sun in Cancer which is ruled by the moon in Gemini. This gives the Child an exceptional chance to struggle for control of the

Figure 32

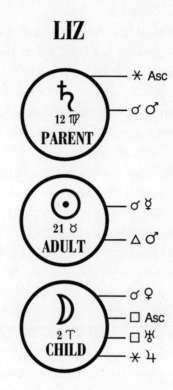

LIZ

Adult, especially when the ruler of Gemini, Mercury in Gemini, is sandwiched between the Moon and Saturn in a tight stellium.

What happened to Vicky was her father. Vicky was an incest victim from age of 12 until she married at 18 in order to leave home. The "contaminated" Parent and Child ego spheres are a major indicator that a distortion in development probably occurred.

Vicky is a most seductive woman; she is coy, flirtatious. She had a problem—she was sleeping with her boss's son. Earlier she had slept with the boss. What should she do? She had seen a shrink but had seduced him, so what good was he?

Eventually the story of her father's seduction of her came out, and how she escaped only through marrying a man who was in the ROTC. Now after many years of marriage her husband was a military officer. They rarely spoke or made love and Vicky had always gone around seducing men. She flirted easily and left the impression that she was excellent in bed, from a purely athletic standpoint. But like a prophylactic, her experience with her father was always coming between her and her life.

The problem is Mercury. Vicky was the most active and articulate incest survivor one could ever meet. She could talk about her problem with great élan. Still, the talk was deceptive for she had never found love, only endless men, proving nothing except that a sexy woman can have certain powers over men, which is what she wanted. It was her payback for what incest had done to her.

The other clues (besides the contaminated Parent and Child spheres) to Vicky's problems are Parent/Child inconjuncts to the ascendant. The ascendant is the expression of the personality, a mask or persona, and when there are many strong inconjuncts to this point, the result is the inability to manifest a confident coordination of inner energies. The inconjuncts come from the Child and the Parent, so a confusion and the need for a lot of adjustment is indicated.

This astrologer kept his distance from Vicky, who might have loved an astrologer's pelt to hang with her other trophies. I referred her to a psychologist and hoped for the best. As an astrologer I do counseling through an ancient craft, not psychotherapy. For Vicky to become whole meant a lot of work with a skilled person seasoned in the problems of incest victims. Vicky's marriage to an older military man and father figure she didn't love but had sex with "once every week or two" while sleeping around with other men was a parallel to the terrible problem she had as a teenager when she was dating young men and yet had a father at home who was sexually molesting her. She

Figure 33

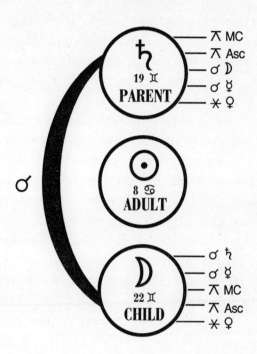

is still in therapy, but has left her husband. She is starting to work through these problems rather than running away from them into a sexual fantasy of power and romance.

What can you do to understand your own sexuality or that of a friend? First, be aware of your Child/Moon's position and sign. As a rule, air signs are more mental, fire signs more immediate, water signs more emotional and intense, and earth signs more grounded. Research your Moon. Who do you know or can find in chart books who has your Moon? Discuss the Moon and its aspects with other astrologically-inclined friends. Consult the explanation of the Moon's powers by sign in Appendix B. These steps will start you down a path of developing awareness.

Further awareness can be generated by taking the time to write down a short history of your sexual education and experience. Who told you about sex? How was it described? What did you think about it before you did it? Were there religious elements involved in the explanation?

What were your first few sexual experiences like? How did this affect your expectations? What kind of partners are you attracting? What kind would you like to attract? Why do you think there is a difference between what you are attracting and what you want?

Go over your Tri-Astral chart and check the Parent ego sphere. Do your Child and Parent spheres aspect the same planets? Are there ways that you are letting parental judgments ruin the joy of your Inner Child? Why?

What type of sex appears in your dream life? Keeping such thoughts in a notebook is very valuable, but it is also very private and great care should be taken to keep your notes confidential. One way to safeguard it is to have a great lock on your filing cabinet; another is to mislabel the file, calling your sexual writings "Notes on Stamp Collection." One woman wrote about herself in the third person and called it a novel. However, if the fear of someone finding your sexual writings is a big issue, then that is something that needs to be dealt with as well. Why is an accurate recollection of your sexual history a problem to have in some safe place?

Make a list of things you like to do in sex and things that you have done that you like least. If you keep repeating some of these bad experiences, ask yourself why. The important issue is that you develop some way of holding an honest mirror up to yourself so that you can grow.

Sexuality is the life force. The sexual act is the passing of the life force. People get pregnant whether they love each other or not when they have sex.

Sex is the act that keeps the whole world going. The mechanism is designed to keep the human race from becoming extinct. Our difficulty is that nature did not blueprint us as readily as other animals. We have free will, and can have sex at will. What a pleasant challenge. There is no mating season; it's open season. Many reams of religious stuff has been written trying to control this urge.

To get in touch with this life force in a meaningful way is to connect to a reality as powerful as the sun in the heavens. To connect with this vitality in a way that allows you to discover the deep, thrilling surges of the life energy as it comes together through two people in union is to enjoy a river of energy that connects one to the infinite. To miss bathing in this river is to miss the true healing of the orgasm, of the release that is central to fulfilling and transcending the human condition. Discovering the biological lightening bolt at the core of sexuality is a journey worthy of the effort, worthy of the study. The rewards of this journey bring two people into a single act that releases a flare from the infinite. When love is added, it becomes the infinite.

Figure 34

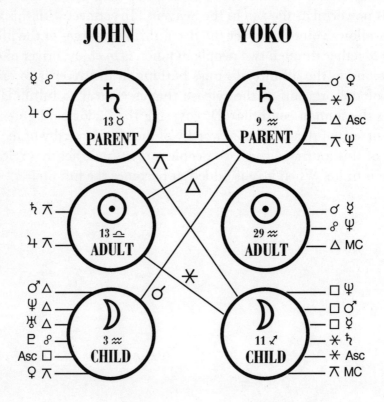

**John Lennon and Yoko Ono
Tri-Astral analysis**

Chapter Six

Two jugglers toss six balls between them.
How long can they keep this up?
Their rhythm must be perfect,
their toss sure to the mark,
they must know each other inside out
they must perform as one.

☆ ★ ☆ ★ ☆ ★ ☆

The Relationship Match: Love All

Who Wrote the Book of Love?

ill this relationship work? What are its strengths and weaknesses? What areas of involvement are important for making a romance viable? Astrologers are asked questions like these every day. Tri-Astral analysis, with its pairing of psychology and astrology, enables one to gain a fresh perspective of relationships by presenting a clear picture of the psychodynamics of each individual's interaction. The two charts interact to show a greater picture. The graphically distinct and emotionally illuminating format clearly shows the emotional energies involved in an easily understandable manner. The chart's adaptability to a variety of methods of evaluating relationships makes it particularly valuable.

In professional astrological circles there are two popular methods of relationship analysis: chart comparison and the construction of the composite chart. The first method, chart comparison, involves looking at both charts and seeing how the planets interact (i.e., his Moon trines her Moon). The second approach, the composite, involves creating one chart based upon planetary midpoints of the two individual charts. This composite chart has its basis in the idea that each of the two planetary pairs (i.e., his Venus and her Venus, or his Mars and her Mars, etc.) merge to become one energy at their midpoint. Thus a synergistic or composite chart can represent the collective personality of the two lovers as a single entity. This chart is then read as a symbolic representation of the dynamics in the relationship. If their collective Moon squares Mars, this couple will argue a lot. If their collective Venus trines Mars, their sexual energy flows well.

Tri-Astral charts are compatible with both of these approaches. In fact, Tri-Astral analysis makes both techniques easier for the new astrologer to understand. The simple, step-by-step logic of constructing and understanding each of these Tri-Astral charts for relationship study will be explained, as well as a review of their strengths and weaknesses.

Chart Comparison

A chart comparison is relatively easy to do. First, it is necessary to have accurate astrological charts for the individuals involved and to convert them into two Tri-Astral charts. Since we have already studied the chart of John Lennon, it is easy to add the chart of Yoko Ono and demonstrate how to construct a Tri-Astral chart comparison.

Figure 34 shows the Tri-Astral charts of John and Yoko in the dual chart comparison format. Yoko's chart was constructed according to the steps given in Chapter 3. Note that the two charts are put side by side so that each of the three ego spheres is directly opposite its counterpart. This makes for a sharp visual aid and enhances the ease of analysis.

The chart comparison compatibility study is a three-step process. First, it is necessary to note the astrological interactions of the ego spheres by major aspect (such as Parent/Saturn square Parent/Saturn). Second, study the strength of the aspect patterns which weigh the ego spheres in each chart. This should yield insights into not only how psychic energy flows within the individuals, but also to how it reacts to outside influences. Finally, combine the astrological interactions of the two sets of ego spheres with the psychological data of weighing the sphere into an evaluative perception as to the way the relationship works (or doesn't work). The overview will show an energy flow that is either harmonic or discordant. Certain spheres will be seen as dominant. Positive or negative energy will reign. This will give the relationship its positive or negative signature. Let's see how all this works with John and Yoko.

John and Yoko

Yoko's ego spheres make very important interactions with John's. Her Saturn trines his Sun, giving him support and encouraging his Adult ego to stretch itself. Both Suns are in the air element—John's in Libra, Yoko's in Aquarius. This adds a mental quality to their interaction, an intellectual way of conceiving things which enables them to approach new ideas and talk about them with intensity and yet detachment. Yoko's Moon or Child ego sphere sextiles Johns Adult (Sun); this encourages Yoko to be playful and John to realize the playful attitude in Adult activities.

The greatest difficulties are in Yoko's Saturn (Parent) being conjunct John's Child (Moon). This leads to a very real fixation on the Parent and Child in the relationship. It is no secret that John had a horrible time adjusting to the way his mother treated him, he had to be raised by an aunt, and that he longed for the types of loving only a mother can give. John withdrew from the world at times and let "Mommy Yoko" run the investments and the household. Also, when the Beatles broke up there were lots of comments that Yoko had some strange power over John. Saturn/Parent conjunct Moon/Child means that Yoko had the type of female Parent archetype in her psychology that could take charge of John's Moon/Child.

The next large problem for John and Yoko was that their Saturns (Parents) square each other. This makes for a lot of mutual criticism and disagreements. Both Saturns are in fixed signs (Taurus and Aquarius) which makes for entrenched differences and slow change. This attraction-repulsion would make them separate once, but the other soft aspects held them together.

John's Saturn (Parent) inconjuncts Yoko's Child (Moon), which means that despite all her power, Yoko feels insecure in the face of John's demands. Yet there is a hidden strength in that both of their Suns or Adult ego spheres are in air signs. While making no aspects to one another, the commonality of elements these Suns share gives their Adults a common mental bonding through the world of ideas.

In summation, both have dominant Child spheres, which makes it fun for them to play together. Both have strong Parent spheres, though Yoko's Parent has softer aspects, meaning she can deal with authority better than John; his Parent has only hard aspects. The real difference is in the Adult sphere. Yoko's Adult has three aspects, one a conjunct to Mercury, enabling her balanced, reasonable side to have some expression, particularly through the trine to the midheaven.

Figure 35

Yoko Ono
John Lennon
Tropical   *Koch*
Composite

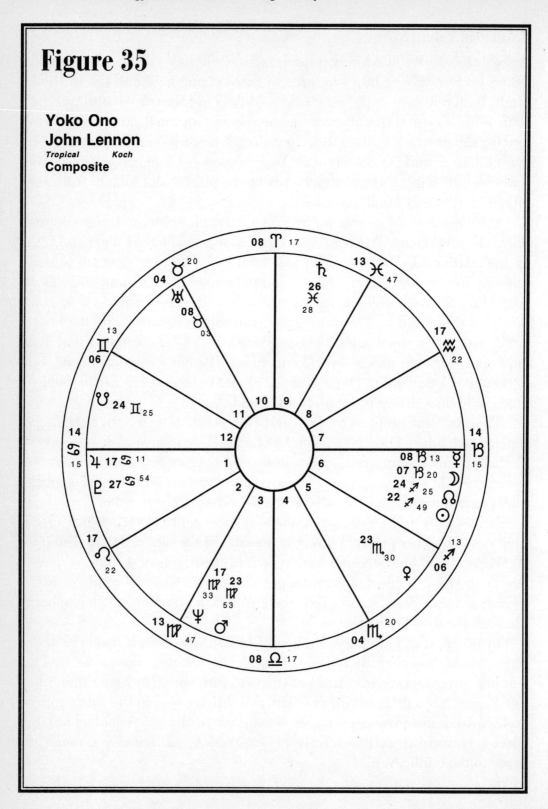

John's Mercury is opposing his Parent, giving him his quick retorts. John's difficulty is that his Adult is expressed through two inconjuncts. This is a weak point because he has trouble adjusting to maturity. He fluctuates between Parent and Child, lecturing us on the problems of the world ("All We Need Is Love," "Give Peace a Chance," "Hey Mr. Tax Man" …), or he amazes us with his ability to be a childlike new age native in Sergeant Pepper's Lonely Hearts Club Band ("Picture yourself on a boat on a river …" etc.). Yoko's Adult is stronger than John's, with conjunctions, oppositions, and trines giving her solid personal power. It is not surprising that John had so much trouble adjusting to post-Beatle life. For him, growing up was a very hard thing to do.

There are a couple of instances in which Yoko's chart is stronger than John's. Note that the word I choose here is "stronger." John clearly has a more creative chart. His tremendously powerful Child is overwhelming. Yoko's Parent conjuncts that Child, giving it support and strength and a strong woman with whom it can interact, to deal with the power of the Child. Yoko's Parent squares John's Parent, giving him the push and the strength he needs to grow. Yoko's Parent explains John's Child to him. Yoko's own Child is excited by the acceptance of John's Adult.

Our overview is that here are two people who have very sharply defined personal interactions. John's Child is nurtured by Yoko's Parent. Yoko's Child is helped by the sextile John's weak Adult which can be gentle toward her. The fact that their Parents are at odds (squared) while they are both children at heart enables a dynamic, artistic partnership to happen. These two are more than lovers, they are artistic co-partners. They Parent each other's artistic Child. John's artistic achievement is unquestioned. Yoko's greatest achievement may be the relationship she gave John. In any event, their charts represent a classic example of a relationship that is artistic, energized, and lasting. And while there will always be some controversy surrounding Yoko as the Voodoo Iron Maiden from the East who broke up the Beatles, the fact remains that John loved her and wanted to sustain his marriage to her.

Composite

Let's see how the composite chart works by looking at the way John and Yoko look together in a combined or composite chart. Figure 35 shows the traditional astrological composite chart of John and Yoko. Remember, this chart is constructed by using the midpoints of planetary pairs. (Note that

John's Saturn is at 13° Taurus, Yoko's at 9° Aquarius, and the midpoint Saturn of the composite chart is 26° Pisces.) While this chart can be generated by hand with a simple calculator from two natal charts, new astrologers are encouraged to get a computer-generated composite chart from a professional astrologer or astrological service.

John and Yoko's composite chart

Figure 36 shows the Tri-Astral presentation of John and Yoko's composite chart. The chart points to the separation of the Child of this relationship from the Adult and Parent. Note that the Child conjuncts Mercury, giving it a strong communicative release. The Child also trines Uranus, giving it great creativity. The square to the midheaven makes—in fact, demands—that this relationship seek publicity.

Thus we can see that for John and Yoko their creative adventures were completely separate from the Adult and Parent functions. At one level they were artistic children.

However, the loaded Parent and Adult spheres tell us another story. The Parent is the dominant sphere; it is dynamic (opposition Mars) and visionary (opposition Neptune). The Parent in Pisces is ruled by Neptune which squares the Adult. The Pisces nature of the Parent gives the qualities of belief, vision, and mind-alternating ability. The trines to the ascendant (Pluto, Venus, and Jupiter) indicate that as a couple Yoko and John had strong rules for each other; their greatest bond was a mutual sharing of benevolent Parental power. It is seen as benevolent because of the predominance of the trines. They shared a common conscience.

It is at the Adult level that this relationship shows signs of stress and strain. The Adult is in Sagittarius, but inconjunct to its ruler. The adventurer doesn't know what to do. There is a desperate quality that the relationship has to be "on" all the time. There is an intensity which cannot be matched by the correct release. The squares to Saturn, Mars, and Neptune push the relationship to its limits. The conjunction to the node gives a fated sense of destiny in the relationship. The lack of a soft or flowing trine or sextile pushes the Adult to prove greatness.

How would we sum up this composite evaluation? The Lennons have a wobbly, fated relationship, if we accept as fate that the strength of the Parent sphere will hold it all together, but not without great challenges and difficulties. This composite chart is a little more pointed in showing the problems that John and Yoko encountered. The judgmental attitudes, the quest for power,

Figure 36

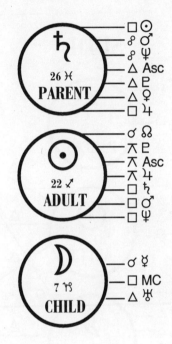

**JOHN AND YOKO
COMPOSITE**

Figure 37

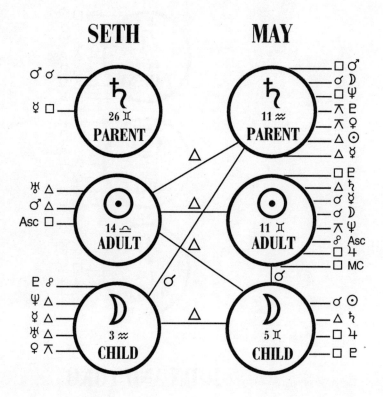

and the drive for a public image all cause problems. Still, the Parental strength in both charts shows that it is through their interlocking need to have a strong and critical person in each of their lives—an individual who can function sometimes as a Parent and sometimes a "wonder child"—that would be their mainstay, their great love, and perhaps even their shadow.

What About Normal People?

Often people complain that books on astrology deal with famous people and not ordinary charts. To correct this oversight we will turn our attention from the world-famous Lennons to two more examples of how to use this method of chart comparison and composite chart analysis. We will use examples from my own files, with the names changed. Let's now take a look at a couple who got married and are still married despite quite an age difference. All their friends had an opinion about their romance. Now you can join the debate.

Seth and May

Figure 37 shows the Tri-Astral charts of Seth and May. The interesting thing is their age difference, 18 years. When Seth first came in for a consultation he seemed like the cat who had swallowed the canary. He couldn't believe his good luck—this woman was young and beautiful. However, of such age differences is the myth of tragedy. Would he wake up one day to discover that he was in bed with Electra, or would his romance end with a younger man stealing away his sweet lady?

Seth is a Hollywood writer. Not a great one, but a working one. He is always pounding out some B-movie destined for a videocassette market overseas. He was popular with the ladies and has consulted with me on a semi-annual basis for several years. He changed women regularly; the longest relationship I had seen Seth have was about two years. At the age of 47 he plopped himself down at my reading table and announced that he loved a woman who was 29. And it was "real" this time.

It might have been easy to have assumed that Seth was destined to have a fling with this young woman, May. Still, to have integrity the charts have to be cast and the astrology studied with impartiality. The stars have to be consulted, not just guessed at with the prejudice of the day.

Seth's chart shows his Child to be dominant. He has a sturdy Adult (two trines and a square). Seth's Parent is the problem; it is isolated with no one to talk to. Mercury is the ruler of the Parent (Saturn in Gemini), squares Saturn, and makes Seth a tough nut to crack. He talks a lot and is critical of every-thing. Once we went to a movie together and he criticized it so loudly, with a writer's running commentary, that the usher came and told him to be quiet.

May's chart has several issues that are good. First, her Mercury is well aspected, trining Saturn and conjoining her Sun; this fact alone will ease Seth's Saturn square Mercury. Here was a woman he could talk to about real problems.

The rest of this chart comparison is classic. Note that May's Parent and Adult trine Seth's Adult. This gives support for real growth. Also, Seth's Adult trines May's Child, indicating that he can assist her in growth as well. Finally, both Child spheres trine each other, indicating easy, natural play between their creative sides.

Note as well how many more planetary contacts May has in her chart than Seth does, except for the Child sphere. This means that May will activate growth in Seth—her Parent and Adult will stimulate him. His active Child means he is younger in many ways than she is.

May is no weak woman. She is a record promoter for a national label and is a big ball of energy. She is tough, with a mouth of her own. At first glance I told Seth that he may have met his match. While May was young, she was a woman who could really have a relationship with him.

Figure 38 shows the Tri-Astral composite chart of Seth and May. Note that the Adult is very strong; the Parent is trine with the Adult, and the Child also relates to the Adult by trine. This combination shows that the relationship has very mature Adult energies directed by a dynamic Parent. Saturn trine Sun and Pluto shows the ability to flow and transform. The opposition of Neptune shows higher vision, and the square to Uranus is the engine seeking freedom and new horizons.

This information made this astrologer tell Seth to wake up and smell the roses. Although May was young, the two of them had fantastic energy between them; to throw this relationship out because of their age differences was fool-ish. Besides, what was wrong with just giving it the same chance he had given the others?

Seth gave it a try with May. One thing led to another and one day they eloped. At age 49 Seth became the father of a baby girl, Margo. Seth still writes B-movies. He stays at home and cares for the baby while May contin-ues to work in marketing. They may seem like an unlikely success story, if one looks only at their age differences, but looking at the Tri-Astral analysis, they

Figure 38

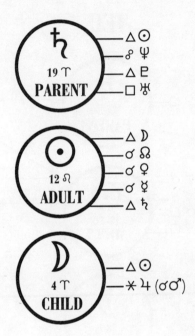

**SETH AND MAY
COMPOSITE**

Figure 39

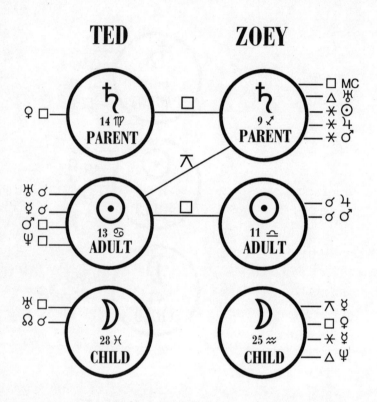

had a great relationship on which to build. And with the birth of baby Margo, Seth seems younger—he has more to live for than ever!

Zoey and Ted

Zoey and Ted (figure 39) are a different story. Zoey had been a client of mine for three years, generally involving questions of career and some romance. A public relations person for a large corporation, Zoey was very pleasant. A mix of Asian and Western backgrounds, she had exotic good looks, loved to dance, and was intelligent. She had no trouble attracting men. It was when she met Ted that she ran into her nemesis, a man who would drive her to truly troubled behavior.

Zoey met Ted at a Los Angeles club. They danced, had a good time, exchanged phone numbers, and made a date for the next weekend. Ted was tall, handsome, intelligent, drove a hot car (which in Los Angeles is very important), and owned his own business as a commodities trader. He belonged to an exclusive club. Zoey thought he was a catch.

From her first consultation with this astrologer Zoey was told that Ted was no catch; in fact, he was an angry (Mars square Sun/Adult), resentful man. Zoey pointed out that they had hot sex. I pointed out that they had already had some sizable fights. The Saturn/Parent square Saturn/Parent of their Tri-Astral charts tells a story of conflict. The Sun/Adult square Sun/Adult adds to the problem—it was as if they were born to torment each other. I suggested that the tension was just too much for Zoey and she should bail out. Zoey was angry at me for the suggestion that she get out of the relationship; Ted would come to love her.

Anytime an I hear a client say that their sexual partner will learn to love him or her, I suspect trouble. Look at Ted. His Saturn/Parent squares Venus, indicating he has real problems in love and sharing. Inventive, no doubt, in the ways of the commodities market, but also neurotic, slow to commit emotionally, and constantly in need of change. Isn't that what commodities traders do—jump from one hot item to the next? His Moon/Child in Pisces is ruled by Neptune square the Sun/Adult making him compulsive, driven, selfish, and regressive. Uranus square the Moon/Child adds to his appetite for emotional change and noncommitment.

While Ted is the more successful financially, Zoey's chart is easily that of the more rounded person. The inconjunct from Zoey's Saturn/Parent to Ted's Sun/Adult only makes Ted more uneasy and more angered by Zoey's attempts to really know him.

The weakness in Zoey, to this astrologer, is Neptune trine Moon/Child. Why is this a weakness? Because it makes Zoey too much of a dreamer, too much of a person who can believe in romantic stories, too much involved with illusion. Zoey's Inner Child believes in Walt Disney endings while living in T. S. Eliot's *The Waste Land*. Zoey's Child cannot relate to the Child of Ted. The Cancer/Libra square of their Adult spheres means that Ted can overwhelm her.

Finally, both Venuses square an ego sphere. Ted's Venus makes him aggressive about women, but not about loving them. Zoey's Venus square to the Child means that she has problems maturing and finding herself. This is a classic case of a man who has ambivalent feelings about women meeting a woman with problems about how she sees herself. The fit couldn't have been worse.

One thing must be said in Ted's favor, he never hit Zoey. But he did drive her crazy, or allowed what madness she had to surface. After putting a rush on Zoey which had her thinking about marriage, Ted dropped her hard for a woman who was more of the country club set. When Ted tired of this woman or when she tired of him, Ted called Zoey.

Zoey forgave this astrologer for all his previous negative advice on Ted and came in for a reading. Was Ted ready for marriage? When this astrologer said no, Zoey was crushed. Being right doesn't always made this astrologer happy. Zoey got back together with Ted, only to be tossed aside this time for a female investment banker with a flair for the polo ponies.

Zoey flipped out. She went crazy. Ted caught her parked outside his place on a stake-out. Instead of being mean, he was kind and told her to leave. She did, but returned to stare in his bedroom window while he was making love to Miss Big Bucks. The police had to take Zoey away. Ted didn't press charges so Zoey was not held, but even the police said they thought Ted was not such a great catch.

Ted in some way enjoyed this kind of emotional play with Zoey, for he alternated between being kind and mean for a year before Zoey cracked up again and entered therapy. Since then she has steered clear of Ted.

It is interesting to note that John and Yoko had Saturn/Parent squaring Saturn/Parent, which is very challenging. However, Yoko and John had several other aspects, Parent trine Adult and Parent conjunct Child. Also, the Child sphere of both John and Yoko had real power to play. Ted doesn't play, he goes on battle maneuvers.

Figure 40 shows the composite chart of Ted and Zoey. As my magician friend, Paul Green, would say, a child of three can see how this works. The

Figure 40

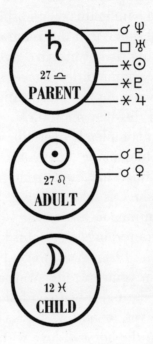

TED AND ZOEY
COMPOSITE

Parent sphere is overpowering. With the conjunction to Neptune, a hard aspect to Uranus, and sextiles to the other aspecting planets, this Parent is the power in the chart. Neptune is important, for it is the ruler of the Child sphere in Pisces. The dreams of the Child are constantly limited by the hard evaluations of the Parent. What type of joy can the Child sphere get if the Parent is always doing an audit of its wishes? What is also to be noted here is the conjunction of Pluto to the Adult sphere. I find this to be a real problem and a foreshadowing of the deep hysterical pain in this relationship. That Venus is conjunct this configuration is the final signal that this relationship will not work.

Ted, at this writing, is not married and has no one living with him, but made a killing in the commodities market in orange juice futures. He's building a house to his own complicated specifications. Imagine how many hearts he'll break as lord of this new mansion.

Zoey had to start completely over. She moved in with a sister and started to figure out what had made Ted cause such a landslide in her life. She worked with a therapist and made some real progress; she is now back at work. At last report she was taking dating slowly, but had found an older man in computer programming as a friend.

One of the important things about this kind of dating disaster is to play the rebound smartly. Don't be in a rush to get back into the swing of things if you have had a trauma in your love life. Wait a while and gain some perspective before you return to dating. When you fall off a horse it might be good to get right back on. However, when love bucks you off, you have to think things out—getting back on the horse of love without knowing how or why it threw you can lead to an even larger tumble later.

How You Can Use These Techniques in Your Own Love Quest

When you or someone you know wants an Tri-Astral chart of their relationship done, take a deep breath, for these are whirling waters. Be careful to take your time and follow some concrete steps before arriving at your conclusion. Focus on the following questions. Have reasons, planetary aspect, and ego sphere weight in your thoughts.

1. What is the energy flow between this person and myself (or between the two people involved) as revealed by the Tri-Astral analysis technique?

2. Is this relationship reasonably within the bounds of being work-able? Be honest. Try to balance the feelings with honest judgment. Try to avoid the build-up and let-down. This syndrome can be defeating and only reinforces negative growth patterns.

3. If it looks good, go ahead. If it looks bad, have the wisdom to pull back and see if maybe you have been kidding yourself. No technique is infallible, but if the signs are very negative the chances are that the experience will be negative.

The chart comparison and composite chart techniques offered by Tri-Astral charts are among the most lucid insights into psychological interaction. The energies of the two individuals involved can be seen immediately and equated as simply as seeing whether or not a picture is square to the wall.

The key to becoming good at using these techniques is to practice, to start a file of charts that you have made. Keep notes on the back as to what happened to the individuals that you studied, along with personal data that may be important. Become a person who uses reason for making astrological decisions. Avoid the desire to satisfy anyone's momentary emotional state with an appeasing view that is not grounded in an astrological technique.

With these simple compass points for evaluation, you will go far and your insights will be solid and purposeful. This knowledge of the ego spheres will open new fields of vision. You will not be looking at the surface of personalities, but at the inner dynamics. With this new map you will see a different landscape, not only in romance, but as we will see in Chapter 7, in your family—where you first learned all about love.

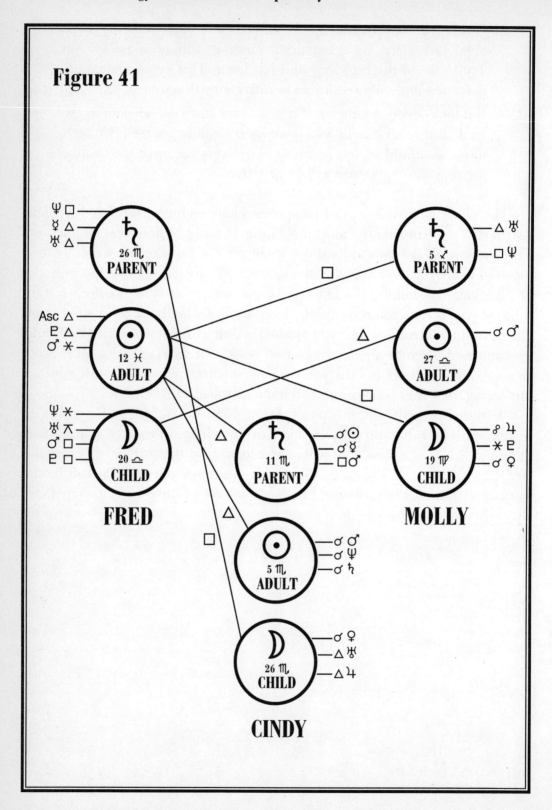

Figure 41

Chapter Seven

The Magician introduces the Human Family.
With a whoop they start to amaze us
with karmic balls of many colors,
all filling the air with oscillating wonder.
So many different sized spheres with different spins!
How can they keep up such juggling without error?
Whoops, a miss! That's the way the ball bounces.

★ ★ ☆ ★ ★ ☆ ★ ★

Tag Team Love—the Family Game All Must Play

Let's Keep It in the Family!

As an astrological consultant, my greatest interest is in the elements that go into the structuring of the personality. What makes a person act in a certain manner? What forces in his or her chart and background made this person act this particular way? With every consultation, these are my basic questions and fundamental approach. The answers usually lie in one word—family. Tell me about your family and we'll discover who you really are, or at least the forces that shaped you as a young sapling. And as the sapling is bent, so grows the tree. Continuing with this metaphor, therapy helps the tree to discover how to grow its own way. How to get "unbent," if you will.

The family is the cradle of life; in its heated emotional environment are forged the basic personality skills and character of those born into it. The biologically fit baby arrives like a type of organic computer, its functioning brain the hardware ready for its psychological programming, the emotional software, to be loaded. The family is our first taste of the psychology of life.

It is here that the baby learns about pleasure and pain, about yes and no—the binary components of all programming. The family: You almost can't get incarnated without one.

The family is a living organism; the whole may be said to be greater than the sum of its parts. There is a polarity instantly at work. The person is at once an individual, a unique self, but also a member of a family, a group with its own needs and agenda. The tension, of course, is caused by the necessity of the individual to conform in some way to the needs of the family in return for food, shelter, and protection. These initial lessons learned at the nurturing breast of Cancer/Moon, so to speak, are difficult to change or reformat because they are the first impressions on the blank slate of the young nervous/emotional system. As that old song goes, the first cut is the deepest.

Studying the family is a complex and complicated endeavor not only because there are more individuals involved, but also that family relationships are what we are born with. In a clear sense of the word, family relationships are karmic because they are unavoidable. As the adage goes, "You can pick your friends, but you can't pick your family."

These are many reasons for the tensions and reactions in the family environment. It is a group dynamic of different related individuals each wanting to live his or her own life. The root of the family, of course, is Mom and Dad, the male and female principle who create it. It is the parents whose marriage and primary relationship are the foundation of the family unit; their emotional overtones will color every other relationship in their brood. Did Mommy and Daddy get along, or did they fight all the time? Such background information alone will enable the astrological counselor to gain insight into the ethos of the individuals who were the product of such a union.

Tri-Astral analysis is a penetrating approach to family study, for it gives important clues and symbolic pictures of the inner nature of this beast with many heads. The key to this approach is the "family circle," which looks at the whole family relationship and will be explained later in this chapter.

First, let's look at one person and his or her parents. You already know the basic principles if you have read the previous chapters. This is the basic triangle—mother, father, and child. This is the first step in your journey to understanding the family.

Basic Father/Mother/Child Triangle

Figure 41 shows the basic triangle which is the first step in studying the astro-psychodynamics of family. Fred is the father; Molly, the mother; Cindy, the child (not their real names). Cindy came to me with a desire to see if astrology could prove that she had been a victim of incest. She had periods of time in her childhood that she could not remember and one of her friends said that such lapses were often a characteristic of incest victims. Although I explained that such a serious situation should be handled by a psychologist with considerable experience, Cindy still wanted me to do the charts, just to see. And let me say that neither I nor the psychologist to whom I referred Cindy found any proof of incest. What both of us found was a dysfunctional family and a considerable amount of abuse on the part of Fred, Cindy's father.

The first real problem in Cindy's life is that Fred and Molly had a very rough marriage. They had two children in a short time, broke up, reunited to have two more children, then separated to finally divorce.

Looking at the astro-analysis basic triangle chart, it is quickly obvious that Fred and Molly would have problems. Fred's Child in Libra relates well enough to Molly's Adult in Libra; however, Molly's Parent in Sagittarius and Child in Virgo are in conflict with Fred's Adult in Pisces. This couple had what we call out west a "feuding and fighting" relationship. Fred drank and ran around; Molly would wait up and give him the riot act. One of their fights left a two-inch scar on Fred's head when Molly clubbed him with a beer bottle.

Looking at Cindy as she plugs into this marriage that shouldn't have been it is clear that she was deeply and emotionally involved with her father. Both her Parent in Scorpio and Adult in Scorpio relate well to his Adult in Pisces. His Parent in Scorpio is the problem. Fred's Parent/Saturn is conjunct her Child/Moon exactly. Cindy's problem is that of many girls who were born first—she felt rejected because she wasn't a boy. She couldn't figure out a way to make her dad happy.

Added to the problem is that Cindy has a very difficult, toxic chart. Her Parent, Adult, and Child are all in Scorpio (this situation is discussed extensively in Chapter 3). The fact that Fred's Saturn/Parent conjuncts her Moon/Child identifies him as the toxic parent in her life. Cindy spent a lot of time rebelling against her father. She borrowed money from him until he wouldn't lend her any more. She tried being a lesbian for a couple of years, and then was very promiscuous with men. With unerring instincts, she married a man Fred hated and divorced him a year later. She was hoping to prove incest to further embarrass the man. Ironically, her mother was hardly ever a topic for conversation. Fred was the show.

Since Fred liked to run around with "loose" women and Cindy became a "loose" woman, I suggested to her that she needed to completely re-educate her Inner Child and suggested psychotherapy, with a counselor she could learn to trust. She took my advice and has been working on this self-awareness and self-improvement project.

Working with Molly was exciting and challenging because she "acted out" her inner life. She didn't just sit back and think about rebelling, she went right out and did it. In the course of counseling her I got the data on the rest of the family, all six members, with birth certificate information. I used this information to construct a family wheel. It proved very helpful in studying the dynamics of Cindy's family.

The family circle chart gives an instant analysis of family relationships. Anyone interested in understanding the dynamics of his or her family (or any other family) will discover that this form of astrological analysis is a wonderfully unique and powerful tool.

Figure 42 shows Cindy's family circle chart. Before proceeding, let's explain how this chart is constructed.

Constructing the Family Circle Chart

1. Draw a circle on a sheet of paper. This is the beginning of your family circle, representing the shared space of the family.

2. Construct two astro-analysis charts for the parents. These are the primary energies in the family. Study them well to get a grasp on the relationship that brought them together. Where were they strong; where were they toxic?

3. Now construct an Tri-Astral chart for each child in the family.

4. Make notes of the different astrological connections that exist between the different ego spheres. This will show the energy flow within the group.

Learning to work with this family circle chart will help you understand the interactions of the household: who was the favored, who was the scapegoat, how Mom and Dad got along.

In studying the family it takes time to see the relationships unfold, even in the symbolic structure of the family circle chart. However, if the reader is

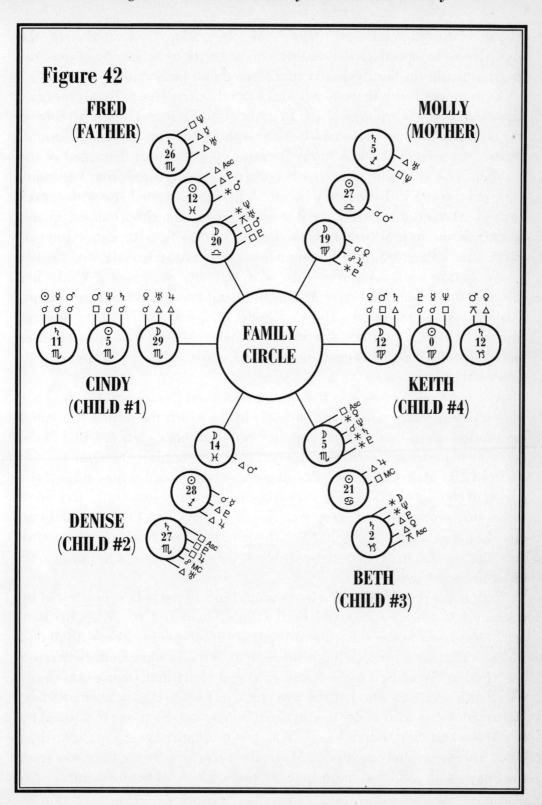

Figure 42

willing to study and follow the web of relationships presented here, the rewards and insight may well enable him or her to understand not only the individual, but the family matrix that formed that individual.

Let's proceed with the analysis of the family circle chart. This is quite an expansion over the triangle chart. In addition to Fred and Molly, all four of the children are now presented in the spheres of consciousness format. Denise, the second child, is to my point of view the most disturbed of the children. She is a lesbian artist who, when not being fired from her many jobs, is involved with women who abuse her. Denise tried sex with a man and got pregnant on her first try. The abortion was somehow messed up and greater feminine problems ensued. Denise has no fit with either Fred or Molly. Fred's Parent/Saturn is conjunct her own Saturn exactly, making her Fred's Saturn return. Surely this is a difficult placement. While her Moon/Child is conjunct Fred's Adult/Sun, it squares Molly's Saturn/Parent. Denise's Sun/Adult squares Molly's Moon/Child, which limited the amount of maternal warmth Denise received. Denise's Moon/Child also opposes Molly's Moon/Child. It is easy to see that Denise has no real rapport with either of her parents.

The toxic relationships to their parents bonded Denise and Cindy. They were trying to make sense out of a home life in which the father drank and ran around. Even though Fred not only inherited money but did well in the automotive business, he was not emotionally there for his daughters.

Fred and Molly separated. But like many toxic couples they missed the poison of conflict to which they were addicted, and after some time decided to stop being separated and start over. To show their sincerity, they had two more children, Beth and Keith. Even though Molly and Fred stayed together only long enough to produce these children, these two were not as not as toxic as Denise and Cindy.

Beth is the third daughter. Her relationship to Fred is best illustrated by the way her Adult/Sun squares Fred's Child/Moon and yet trines his Parent/Saturn. Add to this the wide trine of her Child/Moon to Fred's Adult and we see a relationship which has some tension, but also some flow. Beth never saw the amount of fighting between Fred and Molly that Denise and Cindy did. Beth's problems are that she was still a girl when Daddy wanted a boy. Her relationship with Molly is a strained Sun square Sun, but it is aided by her Moon sextiling Molly's Moon. This is a more manageable pattern than either Denise or Cindy have with Molly. Beth also now lives a long way from her family with a child of her own, close to the family of her husband.

Keith is the fair-haired child—the youngest, the long-awaited son. His Moon/Child is conjunct Molly's moon. His square Moon/Child to Molly's Saturn is offset by the trine his Saturn/Parent has to Molly's Moon/Child. In reality, Molly favors this child and showers him with gifts. The same is true with Fred's relationship to Keith. While Keith's Moon is directly opposite Fred's Sun/Parent, Keith's Saturn/Parent sextiles Fred's Saturn exactly, making it possible for these two males to fight and make up, go to football games together, and even exchange ideas about business, sex, and gambling. Fred's chart is normal in relation to Keith, or as normal as family charts can get.

Compare the problems in the older children's charts with those of Keith and Beth. It is obvious that these two later children have none of the toxic parental involvements that plague Denise and Cindy. If the family has a scapegoat, it is Denise. Notice that Denise's Moon/Child in Pisces is in opposition to the favored Keith's Moon in Virgo (which is also Molly's Moon). Beth has tried to help both her older sisters get over their toxic problems. This help is rejected by Denise and Cindy, because Beth wasn't there when Fred and Molly were acting out the greatest fights of their relationship.

With Denise now living with a lover in New York and Cindy still switching lovers every three to six months in Los Angeles, these older girls have taken the toxins coast-to-coast. Beth is the mother of a daughter and is living out of the country, showing that she had some sort of instinct to "get out of Dodge." Keith is a dandy, a handsome man with lots of lady admirers, who goes from one business adventure to another and has yet to prove himself successful. However, he is very successful with women, and so in certain ways he is a chip off old Fred's block.

The Shoplifting Daughter

Rusty was a single mother who had come to me originally about career and money problems. At the time, she was about to lose her good credit rating because of a car leasing problem, she was unhappy at work, and wanted to know when times would get better. After getting her to pay a lawyer to work out a deal with the car leasing company, we turned our attention toward work. Rusty was in the financial department of a large company. The problem was her boss who had for some reason started to focus on Rusty as the source of the problems in the department. Rusty sought a transfer to another group and was happy with her new working conditions.

About a year later Rusty called. She was very upset. Her daughter, Robin, had just been picked up for shoplifting with another girl. Rusty was really

Figure 43

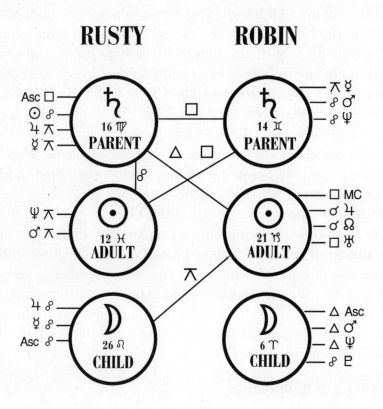

beside herself. She was shocked that this child for whom she had sacrificed so much in terms of work and time and love had now become a common thief. She scheduled a meeting with me for herself and Robin. This type of counseling is not really my strongest area, but I consented, figuring it would be nice to meet Robin and see the person who was, up to now, only a chart on my desk.

Robin turned out to be a very dynamic and aggressively sweet young woman. Figure 43 shows the Tri-Astral chart of her relationship with her mother. The key to Robin's aggressiveness lies in the Child/Moon opposing Pluto which makes her seek power and indicates possible traumatic events in childhood, such as Rusty's divorce from her husband, Robin's father. Robin's Parent opposite Mars shows her temper, her defiance of authority, and her anger toward her father for remarrying and forgetting about her. Her Adult/Sun in Capricorn has no easy aspects except a wide trine to Rusty's Parent/Saturn in Virgo.

The problem is that Robin's Parent/Saturn in Gemini squares both Rusty's Parent/Saturn in Virgo and Adult/Sun in Pisces. This conflict makes it difficult for this mother and daughter to get along, as Robin challenges everything Rusty says.

While it was nice to meet Robin, we did not get a lot accomplished other than getting acquainted. The court had ruled that Robin and Rusty had to go into counseling together for a minimum of six sessions. This proved helpful, but did not solve the problem as much as give both mother and daughter a framework from which to work.

My input here was to Rusty—I felt she had to be wiser, since she was older. The key was to unplug that Saturn square Saturn by encouraging Rusty to stop being so judgmental about her daughter. Robin wouldn't change by meeting her head-on, the powerful oppositions in her chart were made for confrontation. Rather I supported the idea of placating Robin with contractual rules. They would sit down and work out a set of rules and both sign them. Robin could not break the rules, and neither could Rusty. Robin wrote in a rule about being "nagged" to get things done. Rusty wanted the curfew to be met, and more phone calls to let her know where Robin was.

This has helped, but it has not cured everything. Rusty still complains about the young men her daughter dates. However, Robin did graduate from high school, has taken a job in word processing, and is making progress.

The Tattooed Daughter

Figure 44 shows the charts of Harriet and Ruth. Harriet is a very sophisticated woman who has worked hard to get an education and become a psychologist. Harriet initially approached me to do some charts on a few people in her group therapy who were difficult for her to connect with. Eventually, after we had established a relationship through my work on members of her therapy group, Harriet said she'd like me to do charts for her and her daughter.

Ruth is the opposite of her mother. She had no academic drive, little sophistication, and dated men "beneath her station." Ruth was the product of an upper middle-class home. Her father was a successful developer and money was not a problem. However, Harriet and her husband divorced when Ruth was 12. On the surface the divorce was normal—there was some infighting over money and some name calling, but it all died down in a year and life went on.

The problem became acute when Ruth got her first tattoo. Harriet hit the roof over this tattoo, which she viewed as lower-class, destructive, and in poor taste. Ruth responded by getting another tattoo.

Looking at the two charts, Harriet's ego spheres are much more weighted, meaning she is carrying a much larger agenda. Harriet's Parent is very motivated to dominate with the inconjunct to the Moon meaning that play is not to be trusted; the squares to Pluto and Mars give her a temper and a drive for transformation that can be powerful. Her ability to change her life and "pull herself up by her bootstraps" is obvious. The strength of her ego with Mars trining her Sun is potent. Her Child/Moon in Virgo has a strong Mercury trine and Uranus trine to show communication and inventiveness. The conjunction to Neptune shows strong vision, and the Saturn inconjunct indicates that she doesn't trust the elements to get her what she wants in life.

Ruth's Parent in Capricorn makes her a strong, back-room operator. The Saturn trine Mercury as well as trines to Pluto and Sun makes Ruth a person whose conscience is ready for processing data and doing something. She will act out her mental dramas.

Ruth's Adult/Parent squares Harriet's Adult and opposes its own Child in Pisces. The Adult conjoins Pluto, with Mercury opposing the ascendant. The point is that all of these energy points in Ruth empower her to challenge the Adult of Harriet. The two women have different ideas about what a mature vision of life is.

Figure 44

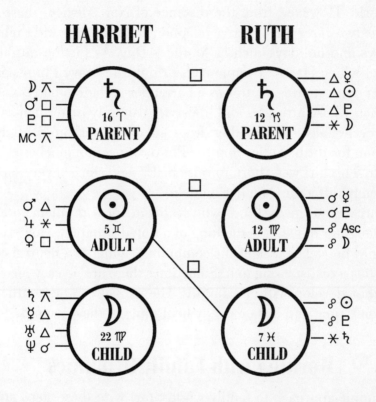

Ruth's Child/Moon is antagonistic to the Adult of both Ruth and Harriet. The sextile to Parent/Saturn enables some reconciliation to her own ego spheres, but not to those of her mother's.

This problem solved itself only when Ruth moved to New Mexico. When the two women had a great distance between them and didn't have to see each other, but conversed only on the phone, the problem eased up. Ruth feels that her mother is a snob, a climber, and social do-gooder who is out of touch with the real world. However, from the distance of New Mexico, these negatives blur and the two carry on an active telephone relationship and exchange gifts on birthdays and holidays such as Mother's Day. As for the tattoos and the "low life" of which Harriet complained, I think the heavy Pluto signature on Ruth's chart points to this. Ruth was a bartender and often had quick encounters with men whose attitudes and life styles can only be termed as Plutonic. Fast motorcycles, alcohol and other drugs, men who get into fist fights—these were common for Ruth. Notice that the Pluto connection touches every sphere of her chart. This girl was "born to raise hell." And she is a very nice woman, just completely different from her mother.

There are undoubtedly those who feel that for a problem to abate only when the daughter moves is something of a failed situation. However, one has to start somewhere. The idea of the combatants going to a neutral corner and cooling off has a realistic ring to it. Sometimes there are no easy answers to the problems that develop within a family. The pressures and conflicts are too deep, and only time and distance may heal some of these wounds.

Working with Family Dynamics

Here is a simple approach to family work. Start with these steps and learn to build your own files on how the family dynamics seem to be functioning.

1. Articulate the problem. For example, Dad drank, my big brother overshadowed me, my mom had a terrible temper, my folks were religious fanatics, whatever. The first step is to be able to talk about it, to get some handles, some vocabulary with which to frame a discussion about it.

2. Discover a way to work with this articulated problem. Figure out how can we get past the shoplifting problem, the tattoos, the thoughts of incest, or whatever the problem is.

3. Discover how this problem affects the client in different ways. Explore why it makes the client so angry. What kinds of reasons

do you see for the responses? The important thing is to listen to the responses. Too often astrologers have a preconceived idea of a problem from the astrological data. The real truth is in the living words of the participants. As one of my friends puts it—their tone always leads you like a trail to the source of the pain.

4. Make a goal of discovering how the client can work with the problem as it affects him or her, and with the problem as it exists in his or her environment.

5. Outline a behavior that will enable the client to work with the problem and develop new growth. Rusty and Robin worked on personal contracts.

6. Try this new behavior.

7. Modify the behavior so that it adjusts to the environment.

8. Keep trying; keep trying.

This list may seem simplistic, but it works only if it is started in good faith and at a basic level. In family work, this is difficult because of the tremendous energy that is released. Shame, guilt, anxiety, and more are at the basic level here. Tri-Astral analysis is useful in that it enables one to cut right to the chase, as it were. The family circle enables one to quickly see family dynamics. The trick is to learn how to use this insight to start experimenting with different behavior patterns.

There is no one answer. There is only a process for looking, seeing, understanding, and changing. Sometimes the obstacles are too great and all solutions are rejected. Sometimes, as with tattooed Ruth, there must be separation. This is better than when separation is rejected and the parties keep fighting at close range and violence occurs.

A key principle is to start at a point of agreement and work from there, no matter how small that point of agreement may be. Harriet and Ruth could at least agree that they loved each other at a distance. Sometimes that isn't possible. Still, except in the most dire circumstances, there is a point at which to begin.

Finally, everything doesn't have to be perfect. An astrological buddy of mine use to fight with his mother constantly about religion. After 20 years they decided to stop fighting about religion and their relationship has greatly improved. They don't talk about religion or astrology. This enables them to spend time together on holidays without screaming at each other about hell and salvation.

The Bradshaw books on the family are of great help here. Do your own research into the wealth of work on the family. Keep researching until you find a model that works. Read books like Dr. Susan Forward's *Toxic Parents*. See how you can plug other perspectives into the family circle diagram. Working in this way you will come to find your way in a very difficult but rewarding area—family.

Chapter Eight

See the Magician crumple paper money!
Tight money wads to juggle just overhead
while the audience watches with glee.
That's real money whirling around up there!
The Magician ends by tossing the money balls
out over the crowd which surges strongly
becoming a sea of outstretched hands.
The weak are being pushed aside!
Real money is what it's all about.

☆ ★ ☆ ★ ☆ ★ ☆

Games with the Boss

The 9-to-5 Dance for the Paycheck

n many ways work is like an extended family. Some of us may often spend more time at the job than at home. Both institutions serve a function. The family unit feeds and protects us while we are small. It gives us role models and kinship roots, including the extended family. And it is the money from our jobs that enables us to buy food and shelter for ourselves, the first step in gaining independence. The umbilical cord of the family is replaced by one of the marketplace. At work there can be mentors, competition, stress, clashes of personality, and even the statically significant possibility of sexual harassment, all of which reflect the emotional entanglements of the family, except from the perspective of the work unit. Yet there is a difference—at work you are paid, and you can walk away if you wish.

The deepest distinction between job and family, of course, is that you can quit a job, but you can't quit a family. In extreme cases one might disown a family, but the roots of the family are deep. Your parents are your parents.

You entered this life through the flesh/gate of a mother. Through your mother you are born into a family who will initiate you, so to speak, into their experiences of life; their perceptions of reality. The family experience you have becomes your emotional foundations.

At the work place it is very important to know how these personal foundations are functioning psychologically, both your own foundations and those of the individuals with whom you are working. Knowledge of how people function at their innermost psychological levels can lead to understanding and good interaction strategy. Learn to be diplomatic and insightful; develop the knack, however awkward at first, to make a studied appraisal of the people with whom you work. Don't look for what you may wish people would be like, look at them for what they are—competitive players with different skill levels and motivations.

The job game is a little like handicapping. The task is to learn to handle different people so that you can advance yourself and play the work game wisely. This is where Tri-Astral analysis can come into play; it can be an important tool in understanding the psychology of the work place. By knowing the Tri-Astral charts of individuals at your job, you can gain insights that will enable you to interface with them at a meaningful level, or at least to develop powerful strategies for interacting with these individuals in a more insightful way.

There are at least three elementary ways of using this celestial psychology on the job.

1. Create charts on supervisors, bosses, or important personnel with whom you work. Check their charts in relation to yours. This will give you insights on your relationship with these individuals so that you interact more effectively. Your Tri-Astral diagram generates a psychological awareness of their major subpersonalities, enabling you to perceive them on a deeper level. You will know which "button" to push and which to leave alone.

2. Create charts of two individuals at the office who may not get along very well and yet with whom you have to work. Look at the areas of conflict and harmony that are indicated in their chart comparison. This will give you insights into their dynamics. If you read the charts carefully, they will give you some insight regarding how to navigate the stormy seas these people generate.

3. Create a work circle with the charts of all the important individuals at work represented. Study their dynamics in a process similar

to that of the family circle presented in Chapter 7. Who are the favorites? Who are the clowns? How do you fit in?

Let's take a look at a very well-known boss and demonstrate how Tri-Astral analysis provides benefits in seeing how to relate to him. First we will perform an analysis of his Tri-Astral chart, then see how this analysis can be used in personal role-playing exercises.

Psyching Out the Boss

Lee Iacoca (figure 45) is a famous American businessman. He is the savior of Chrysler Motors and a familiar character in the long and colorful history of American executives. His blunt, no bull style has made him a media favorite in a sea of corporate blandness. But what if he were your boss? How would you relate to him? How would you begin to figure him out?

Lets take a look at how our celestial analysis would view Mr. Iacoca and the types of strategies it would suggest in interacting with him. His Tri-Astral Parent is Saturn at 3° Scorpio, his Adult is in Libra at 22°, and his Moon is in Taurus at 27°. His elements are water, air, and earth, so he has some balance. Two of his ego spheres are fixed (Saturn and Moon) and his Adult Sun is cardinal—he is a stubborn doer. Let's take a closer look at what the chart presents. As one of my colleagues said about this man, "Here is a Libra with teeth and balls." The joke is that Taurus rules the throat and Scorpio the genital area.

Most importantly, Mr. Iacoca's Parent and Child spheres are in fixed signs, Scorpio and Taurus. This makes him very stubborn and set in his ways. The Scorpio/Taurus, Water/Earth opposition in this instance operates like an tug of war. Both the Child and the Parent in him are very entrenched; play and work are very different things. Notice that at the core of this chart there is an angry Child and a dominant Parent. The Child has no easy aspects. This makes for a childish, ranting temper that is released on enemy authority figures, or employees, which angers the Parent. Mars trine Saturn show that the Parent flows and is a hard worker, but the inconjunct to the Moon shows a uneasy need for control which is backed by the extreme anger of the Child's Moon square Mars.

The Adult ego sphere in Libra of the element air indicates that he is intelligent, negotiating, and a glad-hander. His goal is to reach a concensus; his storminess is motivated in its best sense by the idea that he wants to bring things together and make things happen.

Figure 45

LEE IACOCA

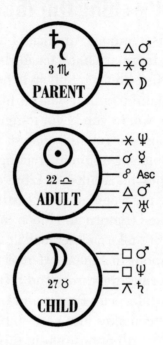

The unique placement of Iacoca's Mars is the key to this man's drive. The Mars trines both the Parent/Saturn and the Adult/Sun. This also holds our first clue to getting along with him as a boss. Iacoca's Mars works well with these two ego spheres. He likes individuals who shoulder responsibility well and who work with harmony. His Adult/Sun opposition to the ascendant means that he will put his professional commitments before his personal needs and will expect his workers to do the same. He has a pragmatic view of beauty (wide sextile of Venus to Parent/Saturn). He is a dynamic speaker and his Mercury is well placed with the Adult/Sun sphere. His Neptune is harmonious with the Adult/Sun in a sextile. He will love to listen to new ideas, to projections of how things can be in the future, and to a positive attitude.

There are two areas where Iacoca is dangerous—the first is his temper, the second is in respect to change. Mars squaring the Moon indicates that this man can fire up in a minute and really let go with a blast. Childish behavior, cry-baby behavior, or being too squeaky a wheel with this man may not get you the grease, but the ax. This, however, is not such a surprise. Iacoca's anger, with his venting at the United Auto Workers, at the Federal Automotive Safety Commission, the Japanese in general, and at certain officials of his own company, is legendary.

What this analysis also reveals is that Iacoca is not as happy about change and innovation as his reputation indicates. Uranus inconjuncts his Adult/Sun sphere and the smart employee working with him will know this is a man who, despite all the changes he made at Chrysler, is suspicious of change. The wise employee would be mindful of this and be careful when suggesting new ways to do things. This is not to say that Iacoca is against change, but that he likes the old order. He rebuilt Chrysler in the 1970s. He worked hard at that, and he was paid well. But even though Chrysler now brags about its safety features and air bags, it is a matter of record that Iacoca fought the government every step of the way in making these changes. Now he acts as if he invented safety bags. Iacoca is also an outspoken opponent of the Japanese penetration of the American market, while at the same time Chrysler has purchased substantial interests in Japanese car companies and it was not until this contradiction was pointed out that Iacoca abated his barrage. One thing he would not want to change is his salary structure, which reflects the old management concept of executive egotism and self-interest.

What does this mean to an employee of Iacoca? If you keep your nose clean, speak positively, and don't advocate wild changes, he is a good boss. But what if you want to advocate change in your group at Chrysler? You have to inundate him with reasons for the change. The man is suspicious of any ideas that do not originate with him. With Neptune square Child/Moon he can be tough on women. He's had ideals and they have let him down. In entertainment circles in Los Angeles it is commonly known that for the "stag" party before his third marriage there were lesbian strippers, and members of the party danced on stage with them to the cheers of the others. This is not to say there isn't a way for a woman to relate successfully to Iacoca, but she has to know what she's doing.

To get along with this boss, you first have to align yourself with his Mars, prove you are a hard worker, and that you are willing to sacrifice a lot for love of team and career. Second, you have to play up to his Venus sextile and show new ideas as timely, good-looking, and of popular value. Third, you have to show that the corporate good is the thrust of the idea. It is the work and the process of making something "fly" that is important. You will compromise, work with others, and see your idea change to become a product of several people, and ultimately Chrysler's, which is to say Iacoca's. Finally, the idea has to have a certain visionary need that only he can sell—Iacoca, "big daddy," is needed for this to work. Then the idea has a chance and you as an employee will be honored.

Astral Role-Playing

The reader/employee may say, "Gee, that looks like a lot of work. How can I do that?" The key is in astral role-playing. The trick is to learn to work and act like a Libra, Iacoca's Adult/Sun sphere. Every one of us has the whole Zodiac within us. Certain parts are more emphasized than others because of the planetary actions. But still, we are born under the entire Zodiac and we can summon up Libra characteristics when necessary.

Astral drama is an area of astrology in which one enters an individual's chart and acts out the energies of the planets in their signs and the aspects they make. I have performed in astral dramas in many occasions. Probably my happiest hour was being Uranus in a drama at the first United Astrological Congress in San Diego. What I learned in astral drama is that is possible to act out an astrological role and to greatly benefit from it. Being Uranus opened me up, and made me feel free and unchained.

To get along with Iacoca, the Libra mode enables you to be flexible, to listen to many points of view, to be smart politically and realize that change takes time, and to be circumspect and get a consensus involved so that you don't stand out and are a potentially greater target for criticism.

Some clients say, "But I have to be me." Not at work, you don't. Work is an environment in which the goal is making money for an organization, and therefore, yourself. You have to assume that you will have to face some compromises. We all act differently with different friends and with different business colleagues as well as with different members of our own family. The point is this: There is a satisfaction versus compromise tension ratio operative here. We need to compromise up to the point where we can bend and flow with some satisfaction. We must play up to Iacoca or whomever as best we can. If we can't compromise, if the demands of an employer are too high and we can't bend, then we must move on. Playing Libra to Iacoca's Adult sphere should work. And remember, it is work. Part of work is your behavior with the authorities who give the assignments as well as doing the work itself. However, if it is not possible to interface easily or morally, we get frustrated. And the fact is there are some bosses with whom we can't work, so we need to change jobs. The reasons for why one stays at a bad job environment tells a lot more about our psychology than if one leaves. By staying we are losing more, really. Why would we choose to lose more by staying, no matter how we rationalize it? It seems that some people need pain.

The Destructive Battle of Egos

One of the first principles of business should be that personal differences shouldn't interfere with the running of the business. However, this often is not the case in the real world of day-to-day business management. The business sections of the nation's great newspapers are filled with stories of boardroom battles, strikes, and personal vendettas that were destructive to the survival of the business.

Norman and Bobby

It was this astrologer's experience to be the adviser to a business that failed because the president and vice president of the company could not get a grip on their relationship. Figure 46 shows the charts of Norman, the president of the business in question, and Bobby, the vice president of marketing (both names have been changed). My personal involvement with this calamity illustrates that an astrologer can do nothing if the client does not follow good advice.

Norman had been in business for himself for some time. His business had grown from a home operation to a thriving concern of 60 people. His wife, Joan, got this astrologer involved in looking not only at their family, but at personnel. Norman tolerated this wifely input and met with me to politely listen to my advice about different staff members.

Looking at Norm's Tri-Astral analysis chart it is easy to see that he is a fun character; his Child is very active. However, Norm's Parent and Adult spheres are contaminated. Norm is great when he gets his own way. Otherwise he is, as one employee put it, "hell on wheels."

When Bobby's birth data was brought as a candidate for vice president, Joan was advised by this astrologer that this was a risky move. Norman himself called me to his office and asked me what I had against such a strong young candidate like Bobby. I replied that Bobby would make Norm the "fall guy." Bobby had a very distorted Child sphere and could be a mean and resentful person. He was a blamer and a resentful Child. Norm laughed; this was a good joke. Bobby was a super salesman and Norm, being a super salesman himself, would certainly know how to handle him.

There were problems with Bobby right from the start. He was a credit card abuser and ran up huge bills on his company American Express card. However, this was offset by Bobby's amazing sales record. Bobby was magic in marketing. Bobby and Norm would have huge fights over Bobby's excesses and his high living, yet they seemed to keep the company going. This went on for four years.

Then Bobby started thinking that he was more important than Norman. Bobby wanted Norm's business. Bobby did not want to be a vice president; he wanted a greater participation in profits. The two men quarreled. Norm was of the opinion that Bobby was a marketing man with no administrative skills. Bobby might talk about leaving and starting his own business, but it was just talk. Norm was convinced that Bobby couldn't run a business.

Bobby then left Norm's business and started one of his own with a partner. Bobby then started stealing all the customers he had brought into Norm's business over to his own. It was a messy war and it cost both individuals dearly in terms of emotional stress, money, and personal pain. The outcome was not satisfactory to either of them. Norm lost control of his business and had to sell out to a competitor. Bobby does still have his business but Norm was right, Bobby had few administrative skills and was involved in a sexual harassment case (often Mars opposite Saturn leads to this distortion of sexual boundaries).

Figure 46

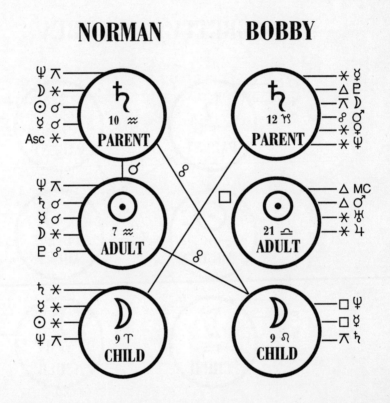

NORMAN   BOBBY

Figure 47

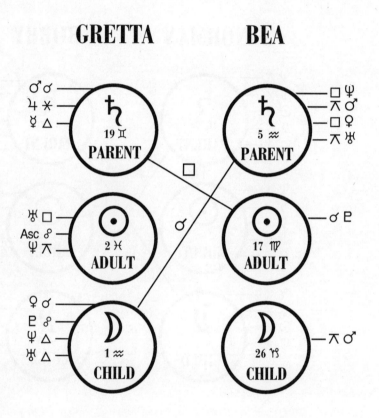

Let's look further at their charts (figure 46) for more detailed analysis. Norman's problem is that with his contaminated Parent/Adult spheres he could not develop the flexibility to deal with the angry Child that Bobby manifested. The credit card abuse and the demands that Bobby presented were really those of an angry Child wanting to vent pent-up feelings to the boss/Parent. Norman was locked into a Parental role and could not get a real grip on dealing with Norm's Child sphere in an mature way. It would have been in Norman's best interest to try to develop a good relationship with Bobby's Adult by re-educating his Child. Norman's inability to successfully manage Bobby set his business back and nearly gave him a heart attack. He currently works out of a single office as a consultant and is making a good living. But he has never forgiven Bobby and refuses to see that he might not have had the problem if he had not hired Bobby or had the insight to manage him with greater perception.

The Judgmental Subordinate

As more and more women enter the marketplace, more women are becoming managers. The value of Tri-Astral analysis is that it is an effective tool with no gender bias. Consider the case of a client who as a manager in a new group at a sizable corporation was having trouble with a female worker.

Gretta and Bea

Figure 47 shows the charts of Gretta, the manager, and Bea, the worker who was causing a lot of tension. Gretta had been hired from the outside to manage this particular group. Bea was a great worker, except that she constantly criticized Gretta, both at meetings and behind Gretta's back. Since Bea was such a strong worker, Gretta was cautious about firing her. Still, it was counterproductive and undermining of Gretta's authority to let Bea be so critical.

Tri-Astral analysis shows the heart of the problem instantly. Bea's Parent/Saturn conjuncts Gretta's Child/Moon sphere. Also Gretta's Parent/Saturn sphere squared Bea's Adult/Sun sphere. The two Adult spheres are in sign opposition, Virgo/Pisces.

Gretta at first approached Bea. It was obvious that Bea could not accept Gretta as an authority figure. She knew she was a good worker and had the attitude of, "If you don't like me, fire me, but I'm not going to let you come in here and start bossing me around." The group manager before Gretta had been a man. Was this the problem?

Gretta had to figure out a way to deal with Bea's stubborn Parent sphere. Gretta finally got the situation resolved not by firing Bea, but by giving her the opportunity to transfer to another group with a male boss. Bea actually took the transfer as a friendly move by Gretta. Once transferred, Bea did not continue to criticize Gretta; she was happy because she had been properly managed.

The point here is not that Bea wanted a male manager, but that she and Gretta had an identifiable conflict which could be resolved so that the productivity of both could continue in the work place.

Some may say that Gretta should have worked things out and learned to work with Bea. This form of thinking comes from the family point of view to the work place—just as we have to work it out at home, we have to work it out at the job. This is a disastrous point of view. We seek liberation though work, not a continuation of some tired family theme.

My advice to Gretta was to devise a lay-off strategy for Bea if she didn't transfer. The woman was a threat—another person could do her job with a different attitude, so why keep her around? She can take her problems to another employer. As it was, the problem did not get to this stage. Everyone was happy, which is what good management is about.

Now that you have seen the above examples of how Tri-Astral techniques can aid you in understanding your relationships with those at work, you should allow yourself to benefit from your knowledge. First, a word of caution. Start a file with the charts of your fellow employees and managers, but keep it at home. Such a file kept at work could prove embarrassing if the contents were inadvertently discovered by an fellow worker. Many people are still very superstitious about astrology and even more don't like to feel they are being studied psychologically. Therefore, keep the notes at home and use the insights at work.

The following are some forms that you may want to use in starting your file (figures 48–50). Use the appropriate form and work with your insights into your fellow workers. Be sure to keep notes about what seems to work better with certain types. Your experience with this work and your ability to develop a "feel" for the formatting process and how the interrelationships can be understood is what is important. Especially important is that old Socratic statement, "To thyself be true." Know your own chart best; know your own strengths and weaknesses. This will enable you to be more realistic in figuring out how you can relate to a fellow employee or manager. If you are consistent in your efforts, correcting your techniques as you go, you will find that your work and management skills will deepen and yield huge pay-offs in real advancement.

Figure 48

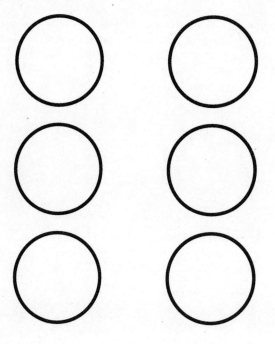

WORKSHEET FOR JOB ENVIRONMENT
ONE-ON-ONE

Figure 49

WORKSHEET FOR JOB ENVIRONMENT TRIANGULATION

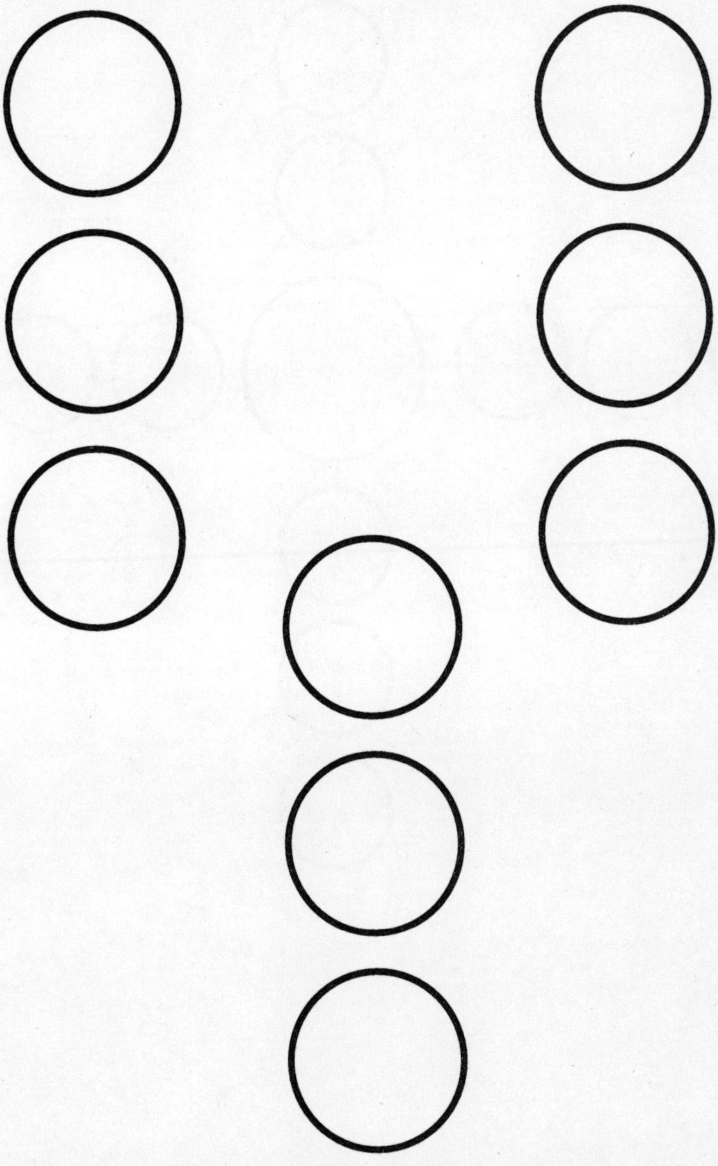

Figure 50

**WORKSHEET FOR
JOB ENVIRONMENT**

FAMILY CIRCLE

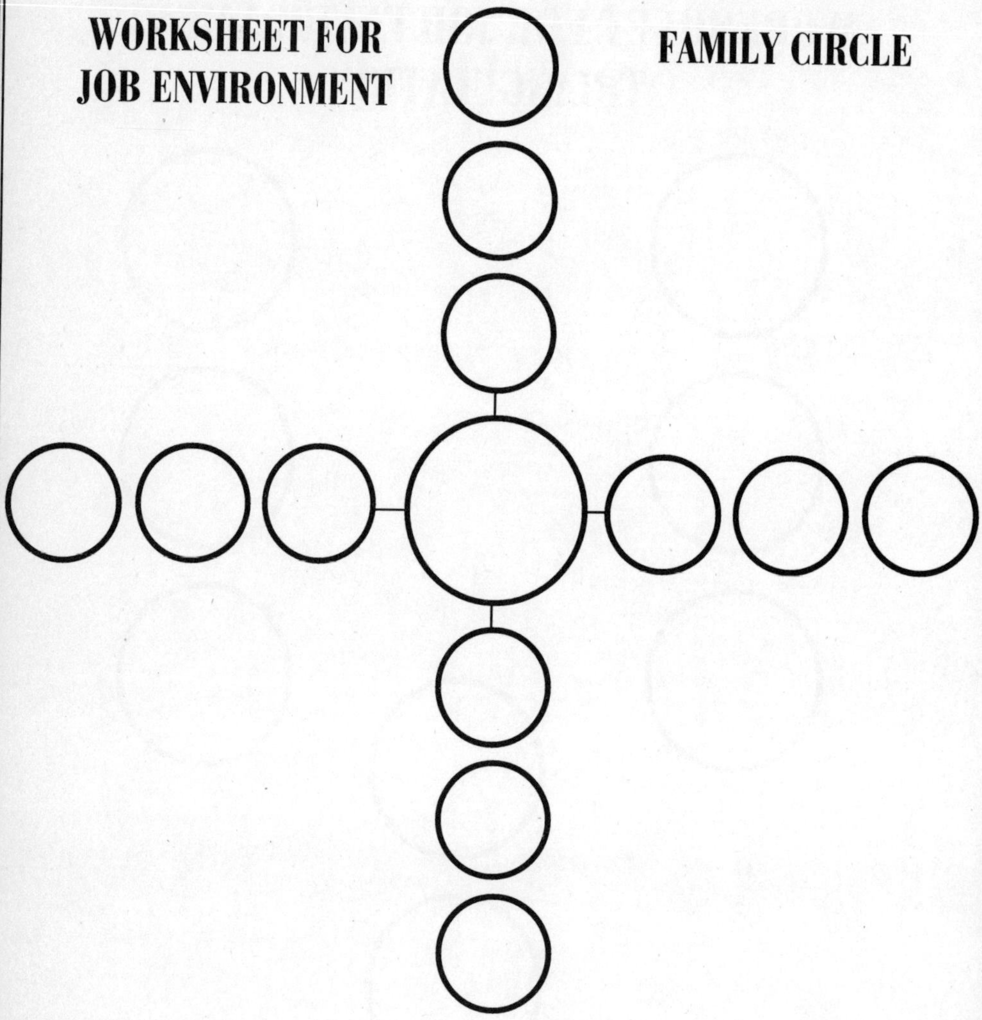

Chapter Nine

See the Magician juggling three round clocks.
They whirl overhead with great precision.
"See how time flies," he jokes.
"Yes, I've got time on my hands," he muses.
The clocks continue to dance in his hands;
The audience cheers time passing before their eyes.
The Magician catches the three clocks and smiles.
"Has time changed me?" he asks. "Every second counts."

☆ ★ ☆ ★ ☆ ★ ☆

Secondary Charts—the Game of Growth

Watching for the Phantom in Your Opera

ow long does my chart last? Doesn't my chart change as I grow older? How often do I need to study my chart? How can I refine the chart with better techniques? Students and clients often ask these questions, because, after all, the birth chart shows the planets at nativity. What about the changes that occur in life? Are these life changes reflected in some way by changes in the chart? The answer is yes. There are a variety of ways to anticipate growth and to sharpen the accuracy of your astro-analysis insights.

For our purposes, we will focus first on the progressed chart. It is a time-honored way to view growth. Progressed charts come in a variety of formats and in a variety of formulations: secondary, solar arc, minor, and tertiary, to mention the most popular. These systems are a field of study in and of themselves. For our purposes, we will look only at what are called secondary progressions, which give an excellent foundation to the world of progressions and a solid basis for understanding psychological growth.

—— ★ **129** ★ ——

Our second technique for anticipating growth is transits. Knowing how transiting planets can relate new meanings to natal charts as well as progressed charts is a good way of anticipating future cycles of growth. It is a logical system which is the backbone of prediction. Indeed, transits are what connect the energy of the natal chart to current events. From the days of the earliest court astrologers on, transits have been a major timing mechanism for planning and anticipating.

This chapter will conclude with a look at what I call "phantoms," a sophisticated way of viewing secondary planetary configurations on the spheres of consciousness. This advanced technique can be used on secondary progressions and transits as well as basic Tri-Astral charts where specially identified planetary configurations indicate that these freelance energies may be lurking.

Let's get started tracking the path of growth!

Secondary Progressions

The first and most important key to remember is that a secondary progression or any other form of chart progression is an intellectual construct and does not replace a basic Tri-Astral chart. Rather it augments the chart by showing what new potentials and challenges may have been added as time makes its mark on the individual. I cannot stress this point enough. The basic natal chart is fundamental to all other forms of progression or transits. The progression simply is an educated approximation of what is likely to happen as time and psychological growth continue.

Thus, with this acknowledged qualification, secondary charts are to be seen as possible plot scenarios unfolding for the individual life. As a teacher I have seen students start progressing their charts to all sorts of dates and starting to worry about imaginary dilemmas. They become concerned not with life in the "now," but what they fear it might be. They are like the hypochondriac who got sick just reading a medical journal, and the punch line is, he nearly died of a misprint!

With this warning now keeping the reader from leaping to premature "progressed" conclusions about the future, let's look at the construction of a secondary progressed chart. In a nutshell, this chart is constructed on the principle that each day in the ephemeris after the date of birth is equal to one year in the growth of that life. To some, this "day-for-a-year" formula seems artificial, and a host of other ways to progress the chart have been presented throughout the history of astrology.

Figure 51

John Lennon
Secondary Progression

Jan 1 1963	17:30:00 GMT
53N25	2W52
Derived Time	
Oct 31 1940	22:59:52 GMT
Tropical *Koch*	*True Node*

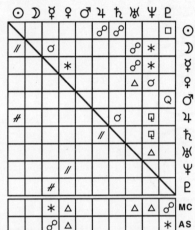

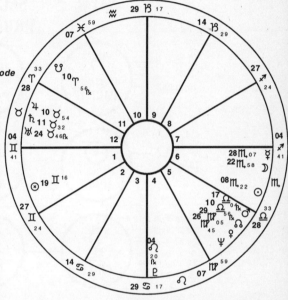

House Cusps

10th	29 ♑ 17	1st	04 ♊ 41	
11th	07 ♓ 59	2nd	27 ♊ 24	
12th	28 ♈ 33	3rd	14 ♋ 29	

Personal Points

	R.A.M.C	301 26	
Medium Coeli	29 ♑ 17	Co Ascendant	04 ♌ 43
Ascendant	04 ♊ 41	Polar Ascendant	18 ♐ 25
Vertex	03 ♑ 09	Equatorial Ascendant	20 ♋ 30

Planets by Sign

1 Fire	1 Cardinal	
5 Earth	7 Fixed	
1 Air	2 Mutable	
3 Water		

Planets by House

3 Life	1 Angular	
3 Substance	3 Succedent	
0 Relationships	6 Cadent	
4 Endings		

	Long	Lat	Decl	R.A.
☉	08 ♏ 22 45	00 N 00	14 S 18	216 00
☽	22 ♏ 58	03 N 30	15 S 07	231 29
☿	28 ♏ 07	02 S 41	22 S 22	235 13
♀	29 ♍ 05	01 N 27	01 N 42	179 44
♂	17 ♎ 04 ℞	00 N 50	05 S 55	196 03
♃	10 ♉ 54	01 S 24	13 N 45	038 55
♄	11 ♉ 32	02 S 38	12 N 46	039 56
♅	24 ♉ 46 ℞	00 S 16	18 N 41	052 29
♆	26 ♍ 45	01 N 12	02 N 24	177 30
♇	04 ♌ 20 ℞	04 N 05	23 N 08	127 43
⚷	01 ♌ 22	07 S 01	13 N 00	122 01
⚴	24 ♎ 05	12 N 02	01 N 51	206 42
⚵	25 ♌ 01	09 S 55	03 N 49	143 59
?	11 ♏ 11	04 N 50	10 S 34	220 16
⚶	19 ♌ 59	01 N 40	16 N 24	142 56

☊ True 10 ♎ 56 ℞   Mean 09 ♎ 24 ℞

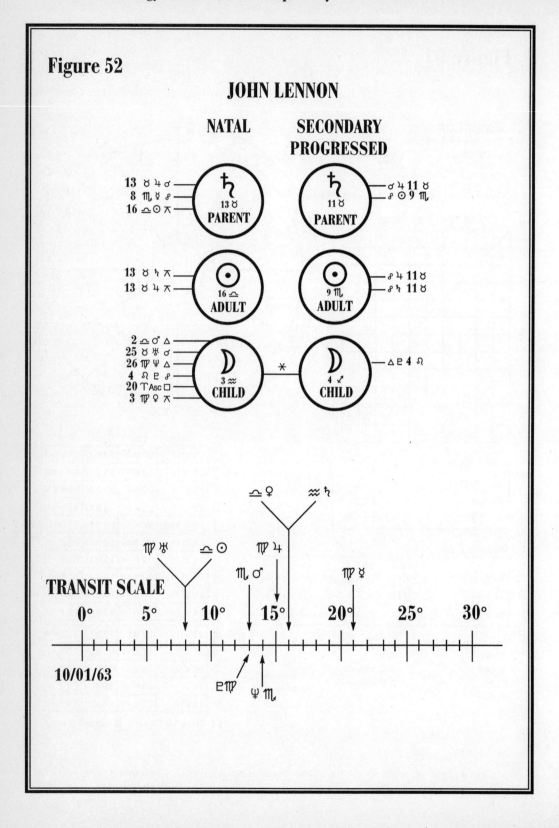

Figure 52

JOHN LENNON

Despite the apparent arbitrary philosophical underpinning of the secondary chart's "day-for-a-year," there is much to be learned by this chart. The first lesson is to work with orbs of only one degree when looking for an active aspect. Tight or exact orbs are the best and only way to achieve the greatest accuracy with this format.

The second lesson is to always have the basic Tri-Astral chart beside the progressed chart so that the influences can be quickly perceived. To demonstrate how this works, let's take a look at John Lennon and suggest that we are in a time machine on the first of October 1963, and John has dropped in for a reading. He and the Beatles are about to start their first big tour of England. They have had a couple of hits and John wants to know what is going to happen next. What kinds of patterns are unfolding for him and where do they seem to be leading?

Let's see what John's secondary chart looks like. We can get this chart from an astrological service or a computer. Let's take a close look. Figure 51 shows the astrological wheel, as one would get it from a computer or as figured by an ephemeris on the day for year formula. Note that by the day-for-a-year formula, John's Sun is now at 9° Scorpio; note that all the planets are now set as they were 23 days after John's birth. Now you can compare this to John's natal chart and see clearly the formula of day-for-a-year. Note that John's retrograde Saturn has actually backed up from its natal position, as has Jupiter. And in this case it symbolically represents the forces of Jupiter's expansion and Saturn's need for discipline and hard work in sustaining the Beatles.

I remember clearly the first time I worked with a secondary progressed chart. When I saw how simple the formula was, I was flabbergasted. A day for a year seemed to pale in the face of a task which, to my eye, needed more complexity. However, after trying several different ways to progress the chart, I realized that there is something intrinsically informative about the secondary chart, especially when it comes to psychological states rather than empirical predictive work. Also, mastering its principles is the logical stepping stone to all other forms of progressed charts with which the reader may want to experiment in the future.

Putting the secondary chart into an Tri-Astral chart format is done by following the same method that we developed earlier when working with the natal wheel. Figure 52 shows the secondary chart on the right with the natal chart on the left. Remember that the orbs must be tight for progressed work. I recommend one degree for either approaching or separating aspects. Some people feel comfortable using one degree for approaching and two for separating, which is stretching it. But since the planets are part of a formula, certainly a variety of orbs might be argued. Some astrologers have different orbs for each planet and luminary. See what works for your sample of charts.

Looking at John's progressed chart you see that the Parent has two aspects, the continuing conjunction of Jupiter and the opposition to the Sun/Adult. The Adult opposes Saturn and Jupiter. The Child has one aspect, the trine to Pluto.

The key to understanding the meaning of this progressed configuration is in the focus and concentration that we see on the psychological level. Note that the Adult has changed signs from Libra to Scorpio. In fact, the Sun is exactly on the position of the natal Mercury, pointing to growth in communication and writing in a very big way.

The ruler of Scorpio, Pluto, in Leo is now being trined by the progressed Child, the Moon in Sagittarius. The Parent and Adult are no longer inconjunct, but are not in opposition. This means John has stopped brooding for a while and is pushing himself to the limits, questing to see where discipline and drive can take him. John's progressed Child, now in Sagittarius, is ruled by Jupiter conjunct Saturn/Parent, underlining the Child's drive to focus its creative and dynamic energies in a disciplined format. This progressed configuration points to a lot of hard work, achievement, and transformation.

A handy way of looking at what is really active in a chart is to study the in-orb aspect flow. This formula can be understood as follows.

Aspect Flow = Hard/Soft/Dense Aspect Ratios

In John's progressed chart he has four hard aspects (oppositions and conjunctions) and one flowing aspect (trine). The dominant aspect flow is with the hard aspects, which means that the dominant energy in John at this time is dynamic, challenging, and pioneering. The impact of this energy is with making something happen, in confronting the status quo.

John, our client, would be counseled that he was about to begin some type of intense transformation; his tour of England will propel him to new limits. The aspect flow indicated a mountain to be climbed and the energy to try.

Looking at the natal chart aspect flow we see four hard, four adjusting (inconjuncts), and three soft (trines). The difficulty of the adjusting aspects is shifting now to a sense of definition (opposition Saturn/Sun). More importantly, the Inner Child who had three soft, two hard, and one adjusting aspect is now clearly focused in a single trine to Pluto—the Child is going to try to transform the man. John the man is going to try to achieve stardom by playing the guitar ("playing" is a Child's term) in a rock band. The trine is applying, giving an outlet for the energy of the hard aspects in the rest of the chart.

This technique of aspect flow analysis is as helpful in sorting out the confusing array of aspects in the progressed chart as in working with natal configurations. The ratio of the three types of aspects always gives a clear picture of the dynamics that are working at the moment of a chart. It provides the key to understanding personal growth.

When you progress your chart or another's chart, always work with the aspect flow ratio. This will give you a sense of the greater picture. Rather than focusing on predictive astrology, try to transcend this inclination by attempting to see the flow of the psychological state. This is the more powerful approach. The state of the mind is the key to the individual's actions. This form of analysis is not hard.

Let's review the steps of working with both the natal and progressed charts so that the growth and flow, the smooth spots and the bumps in the road, jump out at you.

1. List the hard (conjunctions, oppositions, squares), soft (trines, sextiles), and adjusting (inconjuncts) aspects.

2. Compare the ratio of aspects for both charts.

3. Note the change in ratio from the natal chart to the progressed chart. In John Lennon's chart we saw a natal ratio of four hard, four adjusting, and three soft aspects to the progressed ratio of four hard and one soft. The focus on the hard aspects indicates change, a push, a dynamic rush of energy.

4. Look closely at these aspects and try to grasp a mythic symbol from the context of the planetary participants in the aspects in orb. This symbol (or symbols) will give a strong overview of the nature of the psychology of the client. In John we saw the progressed Child/Moon in Sagittarius being ruled by Jupiter conjunct Parent/Saturn, also opposed by the Adult/Sun. This Child/Moon is trined by Pluto. The mythic key that we should grasp is personal transformation through the focused efforts on the Inner Child, though transformation (Pluto), discipline (Saturn), and expanding talent (Jupiter). This mythic context tells the story.

As Carl Jung said, the more we grasp the symbolic interplay of archetypes in our lives, the more we can individuate ourselves. That wasn't hard, was it?

Finally, when dealing with progressed charts (or charts of any kind) remember that the planetary energies and the way they are channeled are not an exact science. It is an art to be a true perceiver of the psyche. The growth of the psyche advances on an inner clock and precise timing of psychological changes should not be attempted except in general terms of the life flow. Eric Ericson said that adolescence, for example, is very hard to track exactly. It starts and ends, but it can be much longer for some than for others. What can you say? Accept the ambiguity and use it to sharpen your perceptions.

Transits

Astrologers often feel most comfortable relating predictable change to transits. Transits are aspects made by the ongoing and ever-changing motion of the planets with respect to the set and specific planetary positions of the natal or progressed charts. The system is easily understandable. Think of two clocks on a wall. At first they are synchronized, then the clock on the left stops at 12:20. That stopped chart is like a natal chart—it is the planets' footprints; it is a frozen moment in time. The clock on the right continues to move as the planets keep moving. However, twice a day the hands of this clock "return" to the position of the stopped clock, or the natal chart. Consider the planets circling the Zodiac in place of a clock's hands and you have transits in a nutshell. This constant motion, the Magician says, keeps us steady.

The direct link between where the planets are at a given time, their physical presence, and their positions in the natal chart gives the expectations of an "as above, so below" interpretation, or at least a synchronistic explanation. A planet may, for example, actually be inconjunct the exact spot of a natal planet. While this activity is often perceived as causal, it is a far stretch to conclude that the planets cause an event to happen. Actually, this is an old scientific point of view. Since Jung's explanation of the psyche and paranormal phenomenon (including astrology), the operative cosmic exegesis is a synchronistic one. After all, the natal planet has long since left that spot and its position is only a point in the sky. For example, Mars conjunct natal Mars means that Mars has returned to the same point in the sky as when the individual was born. Transiting Mars square natal Mars means that Mars is now at a 90° angle to where it was at the individual nativity. Where is the causation of anything in a mere planetary placement, unless it has timing value? Timing is what transits can provide. In any event, it has been my experience that new astrologers have always grasped transits more quickly than progressions because progressions rely on an academic formula.

Transits reveal an immediate link between the individual natal microcosm and the solar system's macrocosm. The daily planetary motion makes aspects happen quickly compared to the motion of the secondary chart. And transiting aspects often can be sharply felt. While usually short term, transits can have a cumulative effect and can signal great change.

Never underestimate the power of a moment. For example, during a time of Jupiter conjunct my Moon/Child I got a letter. It was more than a letter—it was a new thrust of academic life. It informed me that I was accepted to Harvard Graduate School in an experimental graduate degree program, the General Purposes Program. This offer was the beginning of a series of life events that were very important to me.

Not only was the experience of taking my master's degree at Harvard one of great challenge, it also gave me great educational reward. My thesis project was a novel which made a statement about being in the Peace Corps during the war in Vietnam. Obviously, the Jupiter conjunct Moon/Child was a significant transit; Jupiter, the ruler of higher education, signaled my Inner Child's acceptance to Harvard. In a way I consider this book an occult tribute to Harvard's Education School. For what I am teaching here, astrology as part of psychology, is something most schools consider too far-out. Astrology is not yet taught in any form in most academic institutions. I can hear my old graduate adviser, Dr. David Purple, telling me not to worry, to "Go for it"!

John Lennon's Transits

Going back to John Lennon's trip to an astrologer on October 1, 1963, to see what was coming up on his tour of Great Britain, let's look at the bottom of figure 52 which shows you how to set up a view of the transit along with the natal and secondary progressed chart. Take the planetary placements for the day and put them at the 30° scale at the bottom of the page just as you take them out of the ephemeris. This is the way many professional astrologers do it. Enter each planet by degree and sign on the appropriate point of the scale. The number and sign reveal the aspects. The orbs here are tight—a degree approaching, two separating. Let's see how this works.

Things should immediately jump out at you. For example, transiting Venus at 16° Libra is exactly conjunct John's natal Sun, but there is more.

Saturn at 16° Aquarius is trining the transiting Venus and natal Sun, surely a sign of the desire to perform, and to get concrete results. Mars in Scorpio squares the Saturn/Jupiter conjunction in the Parent ego sphere. This challenging energy is an excellent sign of really busting one's buttons. Note that this Mars in Scorpio has just finished conjoining the progressed Adult sphere, indicating that John has a tremendous amount of physical, erotic, and creative energy ready to go on this tour. Transiting Uranus is still in orb to sextile the progressed Adult ego state, giving a real boost in creativity. Transiting Neptune in Scorpio squares the natal Parent, giving the highest motivation.

Transiting Pluto at 13° Virgo exactly sextiles the natal Parent state (and the transiting Mars at 13° Scorpio), showing that the opportunity for transformation is immediate and volcanic. As practitioners of Tri-Astral analysis we can say that it is certainly a strong period in John's life and that the coming tour would be a hit. As a matter of fact, that tour was a rousing success for the Beatles. It was the beginning of Beatlemania where young women would seemingly lose all semblance of decorum and scream their heads off at the very sight of the Beatles.

In summation, transits can be a powerful device for anticipating growth. Too often astrologers look for transits as a source of predictive events rather than as indicators of new pathways for the psyche to explore. Still, when used in the Tri-Astral format, transits can pinpoint areas of the psyche in which energy and growth will occur. The result of a transit should be studied very carefully. It may be an act or an event, but usually the reaction is one of emotions or attitude which then precipitates events. It is in controlling these feeling and emotions that the issue of free will enters the human arena. We can decide to act one way or another in respect to our feelings. Great care should be taken before making decisions.

Always remember that aspects and aspect flow are like the wind. A good sailor has the skill, determination, and willpower to use any wind to get to his or her destination. An inexperienced sailor will have trouble with certain types of weather conditions and should not be active. It is a wise sailor who can sometimes decide to lie low and let the storm blow over. Don't forget—transiting aspects are like the weather, the only given is change. There is nothing wrong in waiting it out for a better day. We have satellites with cameras mapping the clouds every minute, and still we cannot predict the precise movement of the weather. So it is with the human condition. We know a lot, we observe, and still we are surprised at how the weather turns in the human psyche.

Avoiding fatalism is one of the cardinal rules of Tri-Astral analysis. Remember the words of Hamlet—our fault lies not in our stars, but in ourselves in that we are underlings. We can always find some area of choice, even in the darkest hour. And it is out of choice that our will grows strong; through our will we learn to sense the transcendent will acting through creation. Through knowledge of this grand and willful being we become one with the universe and realize our true nature.

It is my thinking that we are all archetypes seeking content. To be aware of your archetype and its components leads to a type of self-realization that makes this life experience a transcendent one. Socrates said it better: "Know thyself."

Phantoms

Phantoms are a phenomena which explain energies or subpersonalities in the Tri-Astral chart that might go undetected. Spotting phantoms requires a technique which uses the Tri-Astral methods at a more refined level. Phantoms come in two basic types:

1. Planets which do not make a primary aspect to an ego sphere, and yet make secondary aspects or configurations to planets with direct aspects to the ego sphere.
2. Planets which make neither secondary nor primary aspects to the ego spheres.

Understanding these two phantoms or free-floating mental energy fields will allow greater focus and comprehension of the astro-psychological dynamics in an individual chart.

Determining the power of the Tri-Astral ego states is important in understanding how these different aspects of our personality interact. Perceiving phantoms is helpful in estimating their varying hidden strengths. The basic technique developed so far to provide such a "ranking procedure" is to weigh Saturn, Sun, and Moon with their primary aspects.

The first refined phantom technique is to extend the weighing process and graphic representation to include secondary aspects, gaining yet another nuance of energy levels. This is done by first noting all the aspects that are made directly to those symbolizing an ego state.

For example, examine figure 53. Mars at 7° Libra squares Saturn at 1° Capricorn. This is considered a primary aspect and Mars is graphically attached to Saturn, the Parent ego state, by a line with a square. However, in looking for phantoms we do not stop here. Aspects to Mars are then noted, as step one of finding phantoms, for these (secondary in relationship to Saturn) aspects reveal more of the true flavor of the Mars square Saturn. Let's say that this Mars which squares Saturn also trines Jupiter at 7° Aquarius. This trine tells us more about the energy flow, for the Mars which squares Saturn has the booster of a Jupiter trine. Let's now add an inconjunct, Mars to Neptune at 12° Pisces, a placement too wide for the sextile to Saturn. The Mars trine Jupiter and Mars inconjunct Neptune represent two different primary aspects to the Mars and are secondary aspects to the Saturn/Parent. The phantom of the these two powerful aspects to Mars will affect the Mars squares with Saturn in a way which calls for careful analysis of the "spin on Mars," for the Mars energy is distorted by the secondary aspects to Jupiter and Neptune.

In the first type of phantom, primary aspects are made by a planet making direct contact to Saturn, Sun, or Moon. Secondary aspects are not directly involved with the Saturn, Sun, and Moon matrix, but are aspects to those planets that are involved with a planet making a primary aspect. Tracing energy back to two levels indicates a deeper understanding of the planetary aspects which focus and shape its nature.

Note that all primary or direct aspects to Saturn, Sun, or Moon are presented by solid lines to the respective ego sphere, and the type of aspect is presented in conventional astrological symbolism: square, trine, etc. To further dramatize and understand the subtle relationships of the energies involved, phantoms and the other planetary (if any) aspects to these planets that make contact with Saturn, Sun, and Moon are diagrammed with dotted lines and are considered secondary influences.

This method can be used to better understand how the inner life is a mix of several competing personality or ego states. In the act of self-individuation, these different states must be integrated into a functioning whole. The primary and secondary aspects to the ego spheres give immediate insight into a new level of influence of the energies vibrating with the ego sphere, and shows how previously uncharted energies—phantoms—can now be seen. The Mars square Saturn in our example is much more powerful and erratic because of the Mars trine to Jupiter; this makes Mars even more powerful and energetic and its challenge to Saturn's structure more difficult to handle for the individual. Yet the inconjunct to Neptune shows a dense and confusing struggle for the correct way to direct the energy of Jupiter/Mars as well

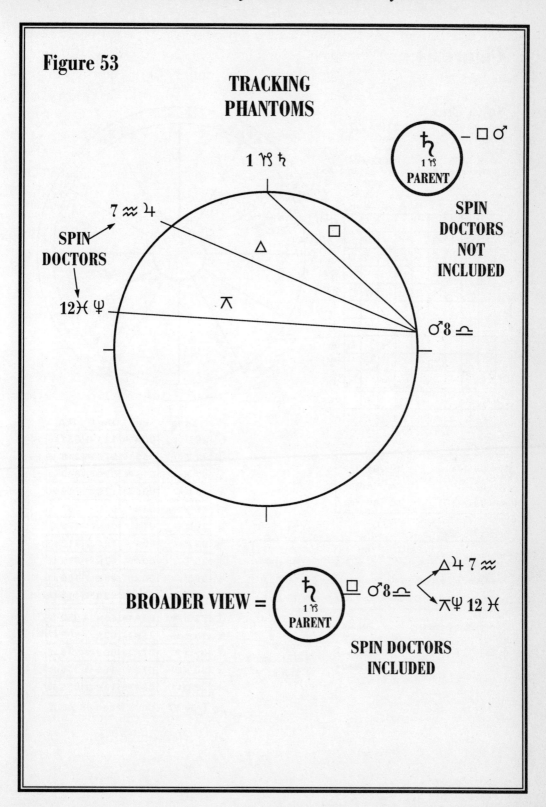

Figure 53

TRACKING
PHANTOMS

Figure 54

Yoko Ono

Feb 18 1933   8:30 PM JST
Tokyo   Japan
35N40   139E45
Feb 18 1933   11:30:00 GMT
Tropical   Koch   True Node

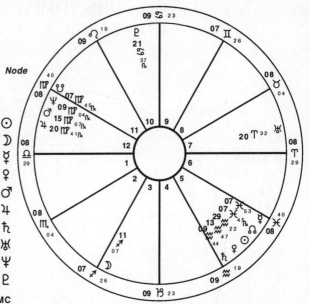

Aspect Grid

	☉	☽	☿	♀	♂	♃	♄	♅	♆	♇	
	♂							☍			☉
	□	✳	□		✳			□			☽
			☍		⊻			☍	⚼		☿
				🝰			♂				♀
	#			♂			♂				♂
						🝰		✳			♃
		//						🝰			♄
									□		♅
	#		//								♆
											♇
🝰	△			Q	🝰		✳			MC
✳	🝰	△				△		⊻		AS

House Cusps

10th	09 ♋ 23	1st	08 ♎ 29
11th	09 ♌ 19	2nd	08 ♏ 04
12th	08 ♍ 40	3rd	07 ♐ 26

Personal Points

	R.A.M.C	**100** 13	
Medium Coeli	09 ♋ 23	Co Ascendant	06 ♎ 56
Ascendant	08 ♎ 29	Polar Ascendant	16 ♈ 02
Vertex	27 ♈ 00	Equatorial Ascendant	11 ♎ 07

Planets by Sign

2 Fire		
3 Earth	2 Cardinal	
3 Air	3 Fixed	
2 Water	5 Mutable	

Planets by House

4 Life	
1 Substance	2 Angular
2 Relationships	4 Succedent
3 Endings	4 Cadent

	Long	Lat	Decl	R.A.
☉	29 ♒ 22 47	00 N 00	11 S 41	331 29
☽	11 ♐ 07	05 S 16	27 S 20	248 44
☿	07 ♓ 53	01 S 20	09 S 51	340 03
♀	13 ♒ 47	00 S 53	17 S 33	316 31
♂	15 ♍ 07 ℞	04 N 15	09 N 47	167 58
♃	20 ♍ 41 ℞	01 N 27	05 N 01	172 01
♄	09 ♒ 44	00 S 34	18 S 22	312 05
♅	20 ♈ 32	00 S 34	07 N 29	019 11
♆	09 ♍ 04 ℞	00 N 51	08 N 57	160 59
♇	21 ♋ 37 ℞	00 N 57	22 N 39	113 32
⚷	23 ♉ 44	03 S 19	15 N 29	052 12
♀	10 ♒ 26	21 N 46	03 N 23	307 07
✵	05 ♏ 50	07 N 33	06 S 20	216 02
?	00 ♓ 29	07 S 30	18 S 18	335 20
⚸	27 ♉ 13	03 S 05	16 N 32	055 40

☊ True 07 ♓ 45 ℞   Mean 08 ♓ 20 ℞

as the challenge of the Saturn/Parent demand for definition and conformity. The result could well be periods of depression alternating with periods of solid work. The client must learn to forgive personal and parental mistakes. While being pressed for action, time must be taken to make room for trial and error. The inconjunct, more than any other aspect, takes time and error to work through. We must all submit to being human and not being perfect sometimes.

The second types of phantoms are very rare. Most planets in a chart make a primary or secondary aspect to the planetary ego spheres. However, some individuals will have planets that make no aspect to either the ego spheres or planets with aspects to the ego spheres. These planets then are true phantoms, energy that does not relate to the primary or secondary axis of the chart and can create effects seemingly out of nowhere.

Yoko Ono

Yoko Ono's chart (figure 54) has a phantom in it. More advanced readers may have noticed a unique quirk to Yoko's natal pattern. Pluto, Uranus, and Jupiter make no direct aspects to any of the ego spheres. It was for this depth of interpretive possibilities that Yoko's chart is so rewarding an astrological subject. Pluto, Uranus, and Jupiter all form aspects with themselves, a tight minor learning triangle in which Jupiter sextiles Pluto and inconjuncts Uranus while Uranus squares Pluto. Where does this triangle fit in the Tri-Astral analysis chart? It is a secondary configuration that can only be handled by the phantom technique.

This configuration gives Yoko a constant hidden restlessness which is fueled by Jupiter seeking to harmonize the Pluto/Uranus square. To see where this phantom will occur in Yoko's psychology, we need to figure out which of the ego spheres it is most likely to influence. The answer is the Child ego sphere, because Jupiter is in a conjunction to Mars which squares the Moon/Child. The Mars relationship to the Saturn/Parent ego sphere is too wide to be considered in orb for an inconjunct. There is an inconjunct between Venus and Mars and Venus is conjunct Saturn, making Venus a secondary receiver of the phantom energy, affecting the Parent in terms of romance and aesthetics. Still, Jupiter's most salient contact is through Mars, which means that Yoko's creative, sexual, and aggressive energy is highly tuned and focused on her Inner Child.

Think what this energy does to the Mars/Moon square! The type of anger and frustration of Yoko's Inner Child is heightened by this exceptional phantom energy that affects her Mars. It is an advanced technique which points to even more evidence for understanding Yoko's great inner drive to succeed, to overcome the obstacles of her youth, and to expand her horizons through a constant artistic evolution and growth through a strong interest in the avant garde. That Mars is also inconjunct with Venus makes her Moon sextile Venus even more important. Aesthetics and beauty were the ways that Yoko found harmony in a life of constant adjustments to two cultures. Yoko has also had an ambivalent attitude about female friends, and the Mars inconjunct explains her problems in this area.

It is important to be able to spot charts like Yoko's which have planets or secondary planetary configurations that function as phantoms—they are there and they are discreetly working, but you have to be able to spot how. By carefully examining the chart and finding how the phantoms can be incorporated into the understanding of the psychological mix, greater insights are possible and a more complete comprehension of the totality of the individual's dynamics reveal themselves.

Remember, the method is everything. Here is a quick two-step phantom test. Make a list of all the planets which make aspects to the ego sphere. Which planets don't make a primary contact? How many make a secondary contact? This reveals the presence of phantoms of the first type. Which, if any, don't make an aspect with the ego spheres of their planets? This may reveal phantoms of the second type. These last planets deserve special attention for their influence and can create hidden or shielded sides to the personality.

You have now worked through the basics of Tri-Astral analysis. Remember that the best results come from practice. So take the theories that have been offered here and put them to work. With a file folder or a notebook, start working on the basic principles so that you can develop your own feeling for working with this still evolving form of astrology. See examples in your own experience of what has been presented here. Test the theories and make your own notes. After a while you will be able to read a chart and develop lucid insights which can guide you through the psychological jungle of this, the final years of the Piscean Age.

Exercises

1. Choose someone—a friend, prominent figure, or celebrity—who seems to have a strange side to their personality and for whom you can get birth data. Construct a Tri-Astral chart of this individual and see if there is a phantom present. Keep a file or list of the examples you discover.

2. Read Jung's *Archetypes of the Collective Unconscious*. What Tri-Astral configurations do you think manifest as these different archetypes, both in a positive and negative way?

3. When reading fiction or going to the movies, try to guess what type of phantoms might be making a character act in a certain way.

Figure 55

ERNEST HEMINGWAY

NAME:
ERNEST HEMINGWAY
BIRTHDAY:
7/21/1899
BIRTH TIME:
8:00 AM
PLACE:
OAK PARK, IL

NATAL DATA:
SUN   28CN32
MOON   9CP55
MERCURY   25LE30
VENUS   13CN08
MARS   20VI33
JUPITER   1SC09
SATURN   17SA49
URANUS   4SA11
NEPTUNE   25GE45
PLUTO   16GE09
MC   3GE22
ASC   7VI34
NODE   29SA17

TRANSIT SCALE

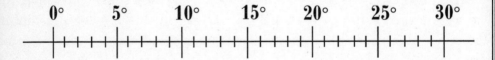

Chapter Ten

See the Magician call famous people
up on stage, collecting their purses
and wallets to juggle high over head.
We clap and scream approval!
This guy can do it to anyone.

★ ☆ ★ ☆ ★ ☆ ★ ☆

Star Trek: Famous Charts for Study

There but for Fortune

here are two reasons for concluding this exploration of Tri-Astral analysis with the charts of famous individuals. First, these charts show the general psychological patterns of individuals who have "made it" in some way in this life, who are in the public eye, and who we know something about. Second, showing them also enables you, the reader, not only to see the dynamics working in these charts but also to compare these "successful" Tri-Astral patterns with charts you have created or will be creating in your own study.

I have elected to offer these charts "workbook-style," that is, with the chart and some space for you to take notes. My analysis of Ernest Hemingway—the American writer who not only changed the way we viewed writers, but who lived as wildly as he wrote—will serve as the first example. After that you are on your own. However, you are by no means bound to the way I do things or even to accept my concept of the aspect flow. While a student at Harvard Graduate School of Education, I studied under John Holt, who advocated "turning the students on to learning, then turning them loose with the subject matter." This is exactly what I am trying to do. You have the basic principles of Tri-Astral analysis in this book. The time has come you for to start flexing your own analytical muscles. This is still an experimental form of astrology and if you wish to share your discoveries with the rest of the "class," write me in care of this publisher and I will get in touch with you.

Ernest Hemingway

Ernest Hemingway is a giant of a writer (figure 55). There is no way to overestimate the influence that this American Nobel Prize winner has had not only on the character of the American novel and the type of hero Hemingway made popular, but also in the character of the writer himself. Hemingway was a writer who was bigger than life, his novels were best-sellers, yet they were also wonderful works of art which delineated stories of great drama. He was a popular writer who was known as a soldier, bull fight aficionado, big-game fisherman, big-game hunter, African safari adventurer, guerrilla war veteran, liberator of Paris, boxing enthusiast, wounded-in-war volunteer, journalist, a lover of women, and the man who coined the phrase "the earth moved."

Here was a writer who struggled to write, who found facing the blank page the most trying challenge of all. He made of the writer a hero who went out into the wilds of experience and came back to write the story truthfully and with clarity, whose sentences are as authentic as a stone fence in Vermont. In his crafted prose we read of men and women seeking a code of conduct, facing that moment of truth, the crisis in experience in which they would discover whether or not they had "grace under pressure."

He was called Papa Hemingway because he was the "grandfather" of younger writers like Mailer, Kerouac, and Kesey. His influence is felt everywhere, including film, television, and journalism. Everyone wants to tell the story with truth, like Papa did.

Yet this is a man who committed suicide, ending his life on his own rather than living on with the pain of skin cancer and other medical problems. I remember once being at a cafe in Paris talking to a young European friend about Hemingway's suicide. My friend said, "He was strong enough to die with honor."

Figure 55 shows us Hemingway's astro-analysis chart. Note that his Parent is the dominant ego sphere. It is this Parent that drove him to prove himself again and again. Note that Pluto is in a tight opposition to the Parent/Saturn. This is the quality that makes Hemingway a compulsive seeker of experiences which deal with death. War, bull fights, hunting, fishing—all these stories have a factor that deals with death. His famous "Death in the Afternoon" tells about more than bull-fighting, it tells of a code by which strong men face danger.

The only release for this stern Parent of Hemingway's is a wide trine to Mercury: his writing. And even in this trine Hemingway struggles to tell the story with truth, to avoid the delusion (Neptune opposing Parent/Saturn) of falsehood and striking his pen deep into the truth. His Parent made him slave to get the story right. It is said that *The Old Man and the Sea* went through 60 drafts. Every word and every comma had to work.

Pappa had trouble with women. Four wives and several women who proudly claim he was their lover attest to this dilemma. Venus inconjunct Saturn and opposing the Moon indicates that dealing with the feminine was a tricky situation for Hemingway. His code worked best for men and tomboys. His fall from national academic favor in the seventies may have been a result of modern women rebelling against his narrow masculine code for the hero.

Hemingway's Adult has two aspects. The first is the Jupiter square which propels him to expand his actions, to challenge the boundaries of his Adult persona. The second is the trine to Uranus that weds him to change, to action, to adventure, to fight for freedom in Spain and France.

Hemingway's Child in Capricorn is ruled by the Parent in Sagittarius. See how this Parent/Saturn has all the power, ruling the Child and the Sun in Cancer. All this Parental influence is what made Hemingway seek a code of heroism; it drove him to constantly judge himself. His father was a successful doctor and Ernest was always trying to prove that he was justified in taking up the writing profession.

His aspect flow ratio is a hard/mutable, a man driven to seek, to move about, to be in action. He had to push, to be where the challenge was. When he went through a series of injuries, not only from his famous ambulance wreck but from a plane crash in Africa in which he was badly burned, Hemingway took his life with a shotgun blast. He made sure the job was done, just as surely as he would take a wounded animal out of its misery.

The Parent/Saturn opposition Pluto would have it no other way. He would rather be dead than unable to live in the honorable way of a heroic man. He left a body of work and lifestyle that has left a significant mark on American literature.

Even when others writers rebelled against his style and his code, they knew they owed something to Papa and had to be good if they sought to be better that Hemingway.

A student of mine once asked me if I would have counseled Hemingway against suicide. I said no. By that late in his life, Hemingway had few options, given his code. And why isn't suicide an honorable way to leave? However, had I the chance to counsel him earlier in his life, I would have tried to get him more in touch with his Venus/Moon problems and develop in himself a more appreciative look at the feminine, not only in women, but that nurturing nature in men that people like Robert Bly are now advocating for men of the late twentieth century.

Time for You Chicks to Fly

There is a raptor (hawk) in England that teaches its chicks to fly in a unique way. Instead of kicking the young ones out of the nest to teach them to wing it, the male raptor flies in with a mouse or other food and hovers above the nest. The chicks go wild at the sight of the food, squawking at their father to drop it to them as he has in the past. Instead, Daddy Raptor lands on a branch just above the chicks. The chicks start flapping their wings, straining up at the food and learning to fly to the process.

What follows, if you will allow this metaphor, is a chance for the readers of this volume to fly on their own. You have all that you need. There are appendices at the end of the book, defining aspects, ego spheres, and other tools of the craft. You have the examples in the chapters of this book. Now the time has come to see how you do on your own!

Consider the following charts of famous people as the raptor's bait, challenging you to fly on your own. The charts are drawn for you. All you have to do is grasp them and digest them. Later you will be able to hunt the game of the psyche on your own, to create your own charts and analyze them. This is the best way that I know to learn. There is the chart and there are your skills. You can only become a hunter by hunting—every raptor knows that. And you become an astrologer by working with charts, on your own, learning by trial and error the secrets of putting everything together to create a meaningful whole.

My advice: be clear in why you think something. Have an aspect that you think is responsible for the character trait you think is operating. For example, Hemingway's temper is symbolized by Mars square Saturn/Parent. Sometimes students have a tendency to toss out an intuitive guess about a chart. This guessing method always leads to flawed thinking. The beauty of astrology is that it works because of the accuracy of the planetary picture, the aspects, elements, and modalities. Do all the ground work first, and know the chart and its aspects well. Astrology becomes a language which will speak psychological truths to you. Remember, in the aspect mix is the key to the puzzle of character. Be a good detective and analyze the evidence. Good hunting!

Oh, yes, I forgot to mention—have fun!

Figure 56

H. ROSS PEROT

NAME:
H. ROSS PEROT
BIRTHDAY:
6/27/30
BIRTH TIME:
05:34 AM
PLACE:
TEXARKANA, TX

NATAL DATA:
SUN	5CN04
MOON	15CN46
MERCURY	16GE22
VENUS	9LE49
MARS	17TA52
JUPITER	0CN07
SATURN	8CP50
URANUS	15AR08
NEPTUNE	1VI20
PLUTO	18CN46
MC	23PI45
ASC	0VI36
NODE	0TA38

TRANSIT SCALE

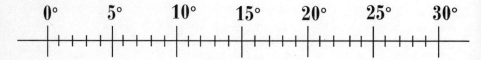

TRI-ASTRAL WORK SHEET

Name: H. Ross Perot

Comments: Why is he called a "little dictator" by detractors? Note his phantom Mercury which gives him such a free mouth. If you want a real thrill, compare his chart to that of the United States. Could this man really be a political leader? Give the aspects that you think support your answer. What does he do for fun? (think water)

Dominant sphere: (this one is too easy)

Aspect flow:

Unusual configurations:

Phantoms:

Biggest strength:

Biggest weakness:

Your personality analysis: Be sure to give the aspect and the sphere configurations. How would you try to relate? Counsel? Befriend?

Figure 57

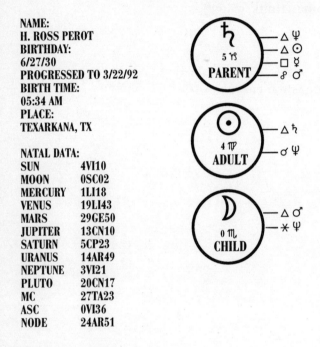

H. ROSS PEROT PROGRESSED
TO "LARRY KING LIVE"

NAME:
H. ROSS PEROT
BIRTHDAY:
6/27/30
PROGRESSED TO 3/22/92
BIRTH TIME:
05:34 AM
PLACE:
TEXARKANA, TX

NATAL DATA:

SUN	4VI10
MOON	0SC02
MERCURY	1LI18
VENUS	19LI43
MARS	29GE50
JUPITER	13CN10
SATURN	5CP23
URANUS	14AR49
NEPTUNE	3VI21
PLUTO	20CN17
MC	27TA23
ASC	0VI36
NODE	24AR51

TRANSIT SCALE

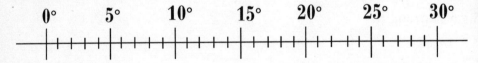

TRI-ASTRAL WORK SHEET

Name: H. Ross Perot, progressed chart

Comments: Chart set at the time of the Larry King announcement of Perot's presidential ambition. Note the Moon is about to change signs. Should we have a candidate elected with Neptune conjunct Adult? Note natal Mercury is still a phantom.

Dominant sphere:

Aspect flow:

Unusual configurations:

Phantoms:

Biggest strength:

Biggest weakness:

Your personality analysis: Be sure to give the aspect and the sphere configurations. How would you try to relate? Counsel? Befriend?

Figure 58

SARAH FERGUSON

NAME:
SARAH FERGUSON
BIRTHDAY:
10/15/59
BIRTH TIME:
9:03AM
PLACE:
LONDON, ENGLAND

NATAL DATA:

SUN	21LI15
MOON	6AR37
MERCURY	9SC15
VENUS	8VI20
MARS	25LI56
JUPITER	1SA50
SATURN	1CP45
URANUS	20LE14
NEPTUNE	6S07
PLUTO	5VI25
MC	7PI01
ASC	18SC13
NODE	13CP11

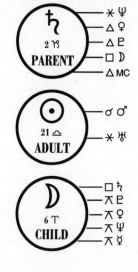

TRANSIT SCALE

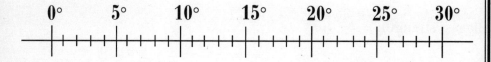

0°   5°   10°   15°   20°   25°   30°

TRI-ASTRAL WORK SHEET

Name: Sarah Ferguson (Fergie)

Comments: What makes her so dynamic? Is she really as wild as the tabloids would have us believe? What is the biggest problem her Adult sphere has to face? Why do Americans adore her so much?

Dominant sphere:

Aspect flow:

Unusual configurations:

Phantoms:

Biggest strength:

Biggest weakness:

Your personality analysis: Be sure to give the aspect and the sphere configurations. How would you try to relate? Counsel? Befriend?

Figure 59

PRINCESS DIANA

NAME:
PRINCESS DIANA
BIRTHDAY:
7/01/61
BIRTH TIME:
18:75 GTM
PLACE:
SANDRINGHAM,
ENGLAND

NATAL DATA:
SUN   9CN39
MOON   25AQ02
MERCURY   3CN12
VENUS   24TA24
MARS   1VI38
JUPITER   5AQ5
SATURN   27CP48
URANUS   23LE20
NEPTUNE   8SC38
PLUTO   6VI27
MC   23LI03
ASC   18SA25
NODE   28LE10

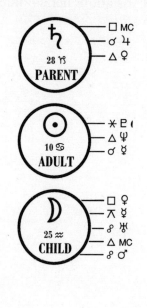

TRANSIT SCALE

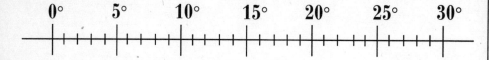

TRI-ASTRAL WORK SHEET

Name: Princess Diana

Comments: Is she tougher than she looks? What aspects say this? What does
Uranus opposing her Child sphere suggest about her personality that could
have made the Royal Family come down on her? Does she long for true
love as suggested by the biographies? What aspects and which ego spheres
support your answer? Does she want another child? What kind of mother
is she? What shapes her moods?

Dominant sphere:

Aspect flow:

Unusual configurations:

Phantoms:

Biggest strength:

Biggest weakness:

Your personality analysis: Be sure to give the aspect and the sphere configurations. How would you try to relate? Counsel? Befriend?

Figure 60

MARGARET THATCHER

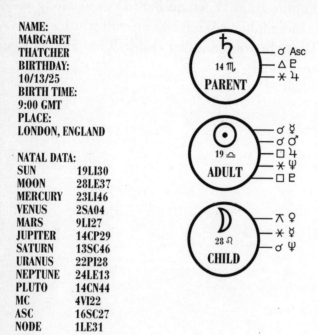

NAME:
MARGARET
THATCHER
BIRTHDAY:
10/13/25
BIRTH TIME:
9:00 GMT
PLACE:
LONDON, ENGLAND

NATAL DATA:

SUN	19LI30
MOON	28LE37
MERCURY	23LI46
VENUS	2SA04
MARS	9LI27
JUPITER	14CP29
SATURN	13SC46
URANUS	22PI28
NEPTUNE	24LE13
PLUTO	14CN44
MC	4VI22
ASC	16SC27
NODE	1LE31

TRANSIT SCALE

TRI-ASTRAL WORK SHEET

Name: Margaret Thatcher

Comments: The Iron Lady is a Libra. Where is the "iron" in this powerful air sign leader? What are the planetary interconnections of the ego spheres that give her personality such a closely woven fabric? How would you get close to her?

Dominant sphere:

Aspect flow:

Unusual configurations:

Phantoms:

Biggest strength:

Biggest weakness:

Your personality analysis: Be sure to give the aspect and the sphere configurations. How would you try to relate? Counsel? Befriend?

Figure 61

STEVEN SPIELBERG

NAME:
STEVEN SPIELBERG
BIRTHDAY:
12/18/46
BIRTH TIME:
6:16 PM
PLACE:
CINCINNATTI, OH

NATAL DATA:
SUN	26SA27
MOON	6SC50
MERCURY	7SA48
VENUS	19SC14
MARS	1CP08
JUPITER	17SC56
SATURN	8LE09
URANUS	19GE29
NEPTUNE	10LI38
PLUTO	13LE06
MC	20PI41
ASC	10CN42
NODE	11GE45

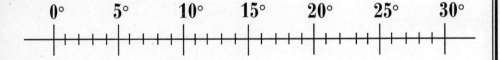

TRANSIT SCALE

0°   5°   10°   15°   20°   25°   30°

TRI-ASTRAL WORK SHEET

Name: Stephen Spielberg

Comments: One of Hollywood's most driven and successful directors. What keeps him so technically innovative? Why does he have to have such control over his projects (give planet, aspect, and ego sphere)? Why is his Mercury in a strong place for a director? Does he ever have real fun, or is he always observing, always making a mental tape for review later?

Dominant sphere:

Aspect flow:

Unusual configurations:

Phantoms:

Biggest strength:

Biggest weakness:

Your personality analysis: Be sure to give the aspect and the sphere configurations. How would you try to relate? Counsel? Befriend?

Figure 62

WOODY ALLEN

NAME:
WOODY ALLEN

BIRTHDAY:
12/01/35
BIRH TIME:
10:55 PM
PLACE:
BRONX, NY

NATAL DATA:
SUN   9SA02
MOON   23AQ59
MERCURY   4SA30
VENUS   22LI53
MARS   26CP06
JUPITER   5SA30
SATURN   4PI01
URANUS   2TA11
NEPTUNE   16VI41
PLUTO   27CN10
MC   24TA31
ASC   0VI08
NODE   13CP11

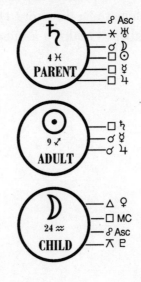

TRANSIT SCALE

TRI-ASTRAL WORK SHEET

Name: Woody Allen

Comments: What attracts Allen to love themes and young women's stories? Is this funny man a happy man (support with aspects and planetary placements)? Compare this chart to Mia Farrow's on the next page. Their Parent spheres make an exact trine. What was the irritant that finally made Woody stray? Hint: the inconjunct will get you in the long run.

Dominant sphere:

Aspect flow:

Unusual configurations:

Phantoms:

Biggest strength:

Biggest weakness:

Your personality analysis: Be sure to give the aspect and the sphere configurations. How would you try to relate? Counsel? Befriend?

Figure 63

MIA FARROW

NAME:
MIA FARROW

BIRTHDAY:
2/09/45
BIRTH TIME:
11:27 AM
PLACE:
LOS ANGELES, CA

NATAL DATA:
SUN	20AQ40
MOON	11CP52
MERCURY	6AQ51
VENUS	7AR51
MARS	26CP26
JUPITER	26VI13
SATURN	4CN22
URANUS	9GE07
NEPTUNE	6LI08
PLUTO	8LE50
MC	0AQ47
ASC	17TA25
NODE	18CN08

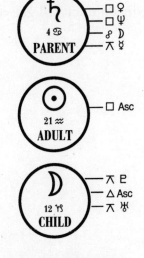

Note ♄/☽ Mutual
Reception

TRANSIT SCALE

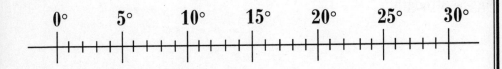

TRI-ASTRAL WORK SHEET

Name: Mia Farrow

Comments: This is the other side of the Woody Allen story with a history that is pure Hollywood. The weak ego sphere is the key to everything. Why would she marry Frank Sinatra, who was 48 when she was 18? Why is she so involved in adopting children? Why is her weakness a great strength as an actress? Will she ever forgive Woody?

Dominant sphere:

Aspect flow:

Unusual configurations:

Phantoms:

Biggest strength:

Biggest weakness:

Your personality analysis: Be sure to give the aspect and the sphere configurations. How would you try to relate? Counsel? Befriend?

Figure 64

JEFFREY DAHMER

NAME:
JEFFREY DAHMER
BIRTHDAY:
5/21/61
BIRTH TIME:
4:34 PM
PLACE:
MILWAUKEE, WI

NATAL DATA:
SUN	0GE48
MOON	19AR55
MERCURY	6GE01
VENUS	22TA12
MARS	8AR03
JUPITER	2CP06
SATURN	17CP56
URANUS	17LE16
NEPTUNE	7SC09
PLUTO	3VI36
MC	23CN16
ASC	19LI26
NODE	22VI24

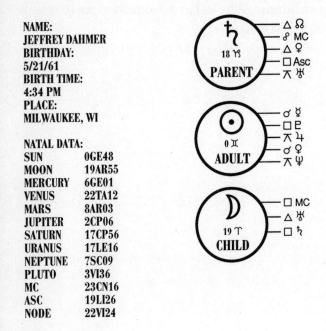

TRANSIT SCALE

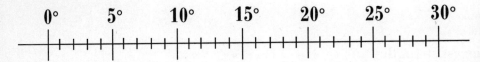

TRI-ASTRAL WORK SHEET

Name: Jeffrey Dahmer

Comments: Mass killer, with that Libra ascendant smile. A classic phantom
Mars in Aries is operative here. Mars's only hard aspect is a square to
Jupiter which is the leg of a yod. Mars also sextiles Mercury and makes a
wide inconjunct to Pluto. That's enough hints. Could you have recognized
him as a bad guy if he moved into the apartment next to you? How? That
powerful phantom creates a dense cover and killer instinct. Why is Parent
square Child also a clue?

Dominant sphere:

Aspect flow:

Unusual configurations:

Phantoms: (draw out)

Biggest strength:

Biggest weakness:

Your personality analysis: Be sure to give the aspect and the sphere configurations. How would you try to relate? Counsel? Befriend?

Figure 65

BOB DYLAN

NAME:
BOB DYLAN
BIRTHDAY:
5/24/41
BIRTH TIME:
27:08 GMT
PLACE:
DULUTH, MN

NATAL DATA:
SUN   3GE30
MOON   21TA30
MERCURY   23GE02
VENUS   12GE59
MARS   5PI58
JUPITER   29TA40
SATURN   20TA04
URANUS   26TA37
NEPTUNE   24VI56
PLUTO   2LE22
MC   17LI50
ASC   20SA19
NODE   29VI53

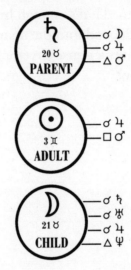

TRANSIT SCALE

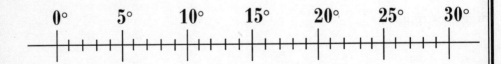

TRI-ASTRAL WORK SHEET

Name: Bob Dylan

Comments: Still riding around on buses performing—why? Is it Neptune that has lead him into some embarrassing situations? Mercury at 23° Gemini is a phantom sextile Neptune. Note the nifty trine of Neptune to Child and Parent. Mercury rules his Adult sphere. What does this mean about his communication skills? Is this man ever happy? Why is it he can sing and write, but his interviews seem so inarticulate?

Dominant sphere:

Aspect flow:

Unusual configurations:

Phantoms:

Biggest strength:

Biggest weakness:

Your personality analysis: Be sure to give the aspect and the sphere configurations. How would you try to relate? Counsel? Befriend?

Figure 66

CHER

NAME:
CHER
BIRTHDAY:
5/20/46
BIRTH TIME:
7:25 AM PST
PLACE:
EL CENTRO, CA

NATAL DATA:
SUN   28TA59
MOON   18CP17
MERCURY   16TA28
VENUS   25GE45
MARS   13LE23
JUPITER   18LI23
SATURN   21CN07
URANUS   16GE25
NEPTUNE   6LI02
PLUTO   09LE36
MC   22PI47
ASC   8CN36
NODE   20PI50

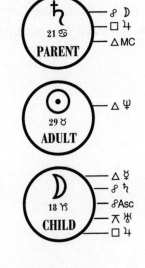

PHANTOM:

♀ ♂ ♇

TRANSIT SCALE

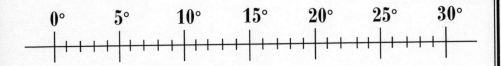

TRI-ASTRAL WORK SHEET

Name: Cher

Comments: Why the tattoos? Where does that voice come from? What indicates her great acting skills? What is the basis of her ongoing rebellion? What aspect and to which sphere could she point to as a promise of success? What does her Inner Child think of her biological mother? What makes her a big spender?

Dominant sphere:

Aspect flow:

Unusual configurations:

Phantoms:

Biggest strength:

Biggest weakness:

Your personality analysis: Be sure to give the aspect and the sphere configurations. How would you try to relate? Counsel? Befriend?

Figure 67

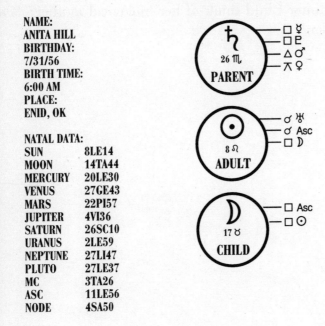

ANITA HILL

NAME:
ANITA HILL
BIRTHDAY:
7/31/56
BIRTH TIME:
6:00 AM
PLACE:
ENID, OK

NATAL DATA:

SUN	8LE14
MOON	14TA44
MERCURY	20LE30
VENUS	27GE43
MARS	22PI57
JUPITER	4VI36
SATURN	26SC10
URANUS	2LE59
NEPTUNE	27LI47
PLUTO	27LE37
MC	3TA26
ASC	11LE56
NODE	4SA50

TRANSIT SCALE

TRI-ASTRAL WORK SHEET

Name: Anita Hill

Comments: The woman who had to speak her say. Loved by liberals; subject to cruel attacks from the right. Take a look at her Moon—this woman doesn't play around. Look at her Parent. Is she capable of lying? Adult conjunct Uranus. Why would you have to bet she'd stand up to the Judiciary Committee? Can you find her "dream phantom"? What is the source of her independence?

Dominant sphere:

Aspect flow:

Unusual configurations:

Phantoms:

Biggest strength:

Biggest weakness:

Your personality analysis: Be sure to give the aspect and the sphere configurations. How would you try to relate? Counsel? Befriend?

Figure 68

HILLARY CLINTON

NAME:
HILLARY CLINTON
BIRTHDAY:
10/26/47
BIRTH TIME:
26:00 GMT
PLACE:
CHICAGO, IL

NATAL DATA:
SUN   2SC48
MOON   29PI11
MERCURY   21SC19
VENUS   16SC51
MARS   14LE15
JUPITER   0SA36
SATURN   21LE20
URANUS   25GE55
NEPTUNE   11LI22
PLUTO   12LE51
MC   5PI07
ASC   29GE50
NODE   23TA32

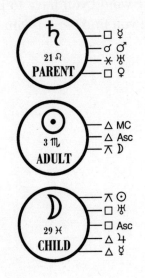

TRANSIT SCALE

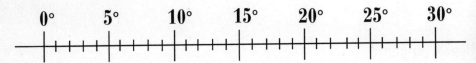

0°   5°   10°   15°   20°   25°   30°

TRI-ASTRAL WORK SHEET

Name: Hillary Clinton

Comments: The first baby-boomer First Lady. Note the ambitious trines from her ascendant and midheaven to her Adult. Child/Moon in Pisces makes an out of sign trine to Jupiter. What does this mean? Mars conjunct the Parent gives her discipline. What gives her the ability to make sharp comebacks? How does she relax? Compare her chart to that of her husband.

Dominant sphere:

Aspect flow:

Unusual configurations:

Phantoms:

Biggest strength:

Biggest weakness:

Your personality analysis: Be sure to give the aspect and the sphere configurations. How would you try to relate? Counsel? Befriend?

Figure 69

BILL CLINTON

NAME:
BILL CLINTON
BIRTHDAY:
8/19/46
BIRTH TIME:
14:85 GMT
PLACE:
HOPE, ARK

NATAL DATA:
SUN   26LE07
MOON   20TA18
MERCURY   7LE36
VENUS   11LI07
MARS   6LI21
JUPITER   23LI13
SATURN   2LE08
URANUS   21GE08
NEPTUNE   6LI51
PLUTO   11LE51
MC   5CN55
ASC   5LI27
NODE   18GE16

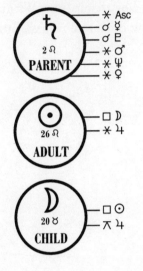

TRANSIT SCALE

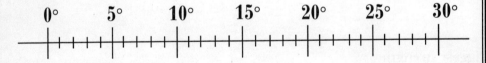

TRI-ASTRAL WORK SHEET

Name: Bill Clinton

Comments: How did this man get to be president? Let's call it a "Leo escapade." What might that mean? Is he a workaholic? What might Child in Taurus mean about his friendships and appointments? All ego spheres are in fixed signs—what might this mean? Why has it been hard for him to learn to be a dynamic speaker? Compare to Hillary's chart and decide for yourself about their marriage.

Dominant sphere:

Aspect flow:

Unusual configurations:

Phantoms:

Biggest strength:

Biggest weakness:

Your personality analysis: Be sure to give the aspect and the sphere configurations. How would you try to relate? Counsel? Befriend?

★ ★ ☆ ☆ ☆ ☆ ★ ★

Generating an Astro-Analysis Chart

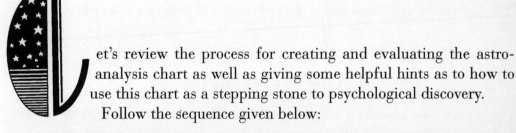 et's review the process for creating and evaluating the astro-analysis chart as well as giving some helpful hints as to how to use this chart as a stepping stone to psychological discovery. Follow the sequence given below:

1. Get the correct date, time, and place of birth of yourself or the individual for whom you are creating the chart.

2. Have an astrological computer center compute an exact chart for you. Or use the chart generation information in a conventional astrology book (available in most libraries or bookstores) to hand-generate the data needed. Some of you may have astrological computer programs on your personal computers. These programs are inexpensive and easy to use.

3. Create a "bare bones" chart with the three rings stacked perpendicularly with the sign and degree of Saturn, Sun, and Moon as the three ego spheres.

4. Look up the meaning of each ego sphere planet in its sign in Appendix B. This gives a basic "feel" for each ego sphere in its "pure" or unaspected climate.

5. Write down all the planets making major aspects (trine, sextile, square, conjunction, inconjunction, and opposition) with each of the ego sphere planets. Attach those planets graphically to the appropriate ego sphere in the astro-analysis chart.

6. Look up the meaning of these planetary aspects in Appendix C and consider the distribution of the aspects to the ego spheres. Then evaluate and rank the three spheres according to the hard, soft, or adjusting qualities that are indicated. It is easy to see which has the most planets aspecting it. Good indicators to begin your study of the ego sphere are:

Which has the most aspects?

Which has the least?

Which has the most hard aspects?

Which has the most soft aspects?

Which has the most adjusting aspects?

If you have any questions about the definitions of these aspects, please review Chapter 2.

Aspect Flow Ratio

The aspect flow ratio is a formula that enables the astro-analyst to see the density and direction of the primary psyche energies and their nature.

The formula is the number of hard/soft/adjusting aspects in relation to the number of cardinal, fixed, or mutable aspects.

This configuration will show the basic mood and flexibility of the person being studied. The more dominant the ratio, the more dominant the aspects and modalities encountered will be. This is an advanced technique explained in Chapter 10.

These questions and ones that you generate will supply the basis for realistic evaluation of the strengths and weaknesses of the ego spheres and will pave the way to an insightful evaluation of the individual's character. If more review is needed, go over the analysis of John Lennon in Chapter 2.

★ ★ ☆ ★ ☆ ★ ★

Major Ego Spheres

★ ★ ☆ ★ ☆ ★ ★

Parent/Saturn Ego Sphere

Super ego: Parent/Saturn ego sphere in the elements and modalities

This ego sphere is composed of Saturn in an element (earth, water, fire, air) and modality (cardinal, fixed, mutable). Consider Saturn to be an energy source and the element and modality to be filters of that energy.

Saturn represents the Parent. In mythology, Saturn was the guardian of the outermost regions. Saturn represents realistic form, accurate timetables, probable outcomes, and the friction in all forms of resistance. Saturn is seen as "Father Time" who puts a lifespan on all things, leading to the decay of all living creatures as part of the life and death cycle.

As the Parent sphere, Saturn represents the rules and regulations that were structured into the ego of an individual as part of the parenting process. Saturn represents survival thinking, knowing where danger lurks, how far one can go, and the development of judgment. Saturn shows the type of self-concept an individual may develop as a part of his or her individuation process.

Saturn/Parent ego in earth: Taurus, Virgo, Capricorn

Saturn is most at home in earth signs, for the planet of structure can most easily build structures in this element.

★ This is especially true of **Capricorn,** which it rules. Individuals with Saturn in an earth sign have a strong and realistic conscience and can be patient and determined, with great analytical skills. In Capricorn there is a strong, commanding presence with the ability to make judgments and act on them. Social and political considerations for any decision are carefully considered.

★ In **Taurus,** the Parent/Saturn ego sphere shows a sensitivity to aesthetics, the joy of possessions and the wisdom of buying good quality, even at greater expense. Expect stubbornness and a strong resistance to change in this Parent. These individuals do not want to deviate from their routine; they enjoy the comfort of old, familiar habits.

★ In **Virgo,** the perfectionist is present; often shy, but still very demanding. There can be strong skills or talents for crafts in these individuals. Look for organizing skills and an awareness of health and hygiene. The most creative of the earth Saturn positions, the spectrum is wide. A surgeon, inventor, documentary film-maker, or computer whiz may have this Parent.

Saturn/Parent ego in water: Cancer, Scorpio, Pisces

Saturn in water is tricky; the fluid nature of this element cannot be structured as in earth which is solid and definable. In water, Saturn must seek to work in currents, in controlling temperature, in seeking clarity in a medium which can become quickly cloudy. Saturn can be almost irrational in water.

★ In **Cancer,** the Parent is a strict disciplinarian. Strong defense mechanisms can create a subjective individual. Feelings of loyalty and worth must be earned. This Parent can be very jealous, have strong intuitions, and can be psychic. Very subjective feelings about money and possessions can lead to unusual investments or methods of saving. Ruthless defender of family or personal pride.

★ In **Scorpio,** the Parent has great emotional intensity and is given to secrecy and shrewdness. Can be vindictive if slighted. Strong fixations on power and money with an equal interest in power and sex. Can love or hate with great zeal. Excellent intuition and good for investigations. Pain is seen as the great teacher; the purifier. Can withdraw love or attention as a form of punishment.

✦ In **Pisces,** the Parent/Saturn has difficulty projecting form in this sign that represents the highs and lows of the spiritual world, as well as the decaying transformation of the cosmos. This Parent holds on to the past for too long, trying to resist what must be accepted. There is a strong sense of guilt in thinking about what might have been rather than accepting what is coming now. A strong sense of intuition and a willingness to go with the flow into the future are what is needed here. Irrational fears can be forgotten. Remember the two fish—one is going up and the other down. This Parent must look up.

Saturn/Parent ego in fire: Aries, Leo, Sagittarius

The Parent/Saturn in fire has to do with control of the flame and how to keep the fire burning warmly and productively, but not out of control in a conflagration of anger or blind passion.

✦ Parent/Saturn in **Aries** inhibits the flow of the energies of life. The individual is good at debate, challenging authority, and questioning the status quo. There are strong parental fixations, potential conflicts, and suspicions of orders. This Parent has good concentration and the ability to push the body in competition.

✦ Parent/Saturn in **Leo** often needs to learn to be less selfish. Very strong will makes for a powerful individual with strong leadership potential. Personal pride often gets in the way of love. Fixed nature of the sign means the energy to persist is present. A great personal warmth must be backed with a true ability to see the other person's point of view.

✦ Parent/Saturn in **Sagittarius** is a good teacher and respects individual rights. There is an interest in the unusual and the different. Look for blunt honesty and a scientific attitude. The issues of religion are met with open enthusiasm for discussion and debate. There can be strong biases when the Parent is afflicted, creating an extremist who feels the divine answer has arrived. Pride is second only to that of Leo.

Parent/Saturn ego in air: Gemini, Libra, Aquarius

Parent/Saturn in air reveals a mental state and the structuring architectural forming of thoughtful castles in the air.

⋆ Parent in **Gemini** has to watch out for biting off more than the mind can chew. Saturn slows down Gemini's racing mental processes, which makes this a place where polarities can possibly be seen and understood. Teaching and communications are strong talents, as are assembling information and "buzzwords" about knowledge. Usually these individuals can find something to talk about with anyone. If the Saturn is well placed they can go into deep subjects; if afflicted, they will skim the surface.

⋆ Parent in **Libra** has very strong judgment and an especially discriminating ethical eye. Their drive for perfection makes them difficult to understand. In relationships there is a strong diplomatic flair which can at times be seen as very formal or preconceived. They are clever at seeking consensus and seem to stay in control. One-on-one, their demanding needs for high performance and potentially snobby nature makes them candidates for high blood pressure. They need to cut themselves some slack and realize that perfection is hard to achieve.

⋆ Parent/Saturn in **Aquarius:** impersonal and unemotional; concerned with the structure of ideas and observations. Consummate philosopher and psychologist. Has difficulty with criticism or changes. Willing to look at the unusual. Wants to make order from chaos. Has difficulty admitting a mistake. Demands perfection in thinking.

Adult/Sun Ego Sphere

The Sun represents the core of the individual, the adult consciousness to which the self is constantly evolving. The sun is the power, sign, element, and modality that filters this radiant energy into a way of manifesting a celestial environment. While the sun exists, it does not exist to us except through a sign, just as an ego does not exist except in an incarnate body.

The element and modality of the sign indicates the grounding orientation of the adult ego, which is to say the outlook which makes the adult feel most individuated and self-aware.

Adult/Sun ego in earth: Taurus, Virgo, Capricorn

✶ Adult/Sun in **Taurus** is a stable person who is thorough and patient. This individual is practical and artistic with a strong sense of sensuality. Friendship is highly prized and there is great loyalty and affection. Sometimes though to be self-indulgent or even stubborn, there is a flair for the material world. The phrase "looking good means feeling good" seems to apply. Greed is not an unknown trait, but is usually modified into an ambitious drive to achieve and acquire the good life. Durability and persistence find manifestation here.

✶ Adult/Sun in **Virgo** is a practical individual. This ego state loves to analyze things. They are industrious and studious. They may feel that they invented the scientific method of methodical thinking and observation. They are humane and discriminating. They can appear overly critical at times, sometimes involved in petty details. While usually considered the cleanest of ego sphere positions, there is nothing sloppier than a Virgo gone melancholy. They don't seem to trust what they can't analyze and can be pedantic. On the whole, they love what engages their minds.

✶ Adult/Sun in **Capricorn** seeks to climb high with strong ambition. There is a real quality of utilitarianism to this ego state. The individual is cautious and responsible, sometimes even domineering, and filled with conventional wisdom with a knack for business. Often very picky and economical, these people are hardworking and serious. They can be inhibited and look to material goods for status. Their emotions take a back seat to reason and they pride themselves on their traditional values.

Adult/Sun ego in water: Cancer, Scorpio, Pisces

✶ Adult/Sun in **Cancer** is a tenacious person whose deep subjective love of life reveals a sensitive and emotional nature. Often very domestic, these individuals are the nurturers of the family of humanity. They are intuitive and artistic, with strong but eccentric drives towards money. They can be manipulative and have a strong temper, especially in the defense of loved ones. Their feelings can be easily hurt, and then they brood. They are patriotic, country being an extension of home. They have strong episodic memories and are epic storytellers. They have a deep devotion to life, their gods, and their home.

⋆ Adult/Sun in **Scorpio** gives an intensity to all activities. Strong on sexuality and power, these individuals are resourceful and great at investigations and getting to the bottom of any idea, person, place, or thing. Their strong passions can breed a jealous side as well as a secretive and temperamental streak. Like all fixed signs, they are slow to change their minds and hold stubbornly to what they feel is right, even in the face of criticism. Their barbed wits have the sting of the scorpion, due to an awareness that seems to have x-ray vision. Never underestimate their desire or resourcefulness.

⋆ Adult/Sun in **Pisces** is a compassionate, understanding person. Remember there are two fish to Pisces, a dual sign. One fish is going up, or taking the high road, and the other is going down. The split is between the high road of the spirit and high ideas, and the low road of substance abuse and self-pity. Generally, these individuals have a strong sense of music and are intuitive and emotional. Their capacity for great belief makes these the people who can perform miracles. There is an impractical side to this sign that doesn't want to be caught up in the small details, but only the big picture. Traditionally thought to be a psychic sign, they will often have flashes of insight. Artistic, their sense of color and tone are unmatched.

Adult/Sun ego in fire: Aries, Leo, Sagittarius

⋆ Adult/Sun in **Aries** is bold and competitive. These individuals trust their impulses and are eager to get things going. They live in the now and are dynamic and independent. They have strong, quick minds and the courage of their convictions. They can be pushy and domineering if they feel someone is slowing them down or standing in the way. There is a distinct self-interest at work; the key is to align oneself with them and let them charge the castle wall. Detail work can bore them. Their quick-tempered natures may be overplayed in some books, but they are not afraid of confrontations.

⋆ Adult/Sun in **Leo** is the sign of a magnetic individual who is dramatic and proud. This ego sphere is ambitious, romantic, and optimistic. They have a certain dignity and carriage to them that is easy to spot. A fixed sign, they are strong in perseverance and are self-assured, sometimes leaning to the autocratic. Creative and with a flare for the theatrical, they can border on being status conscious and pretentious. The ego is strong; vanity can sometimes eclipse common sense.

⋆ Adult/Sun in **Sagittarius** is straight-forward. These individuals will tell it like it is. Sometimes criticized for being blunt and impatient, this fire sign is one that likes to "call them like I see them." Freedom-loving, high-minded, sometimes a gambler, these individuals are broad-minded and enthusiastic. They can be impatient and pushy, but that is because they perceive the fruit is dying on the vine, and the time has come to act. Religious, but not necessary traditional, these individuals are philosophical. They can become hot-headed over injustices and try to get others to visualize a better world.

Adult/Sun ego in air: Gemini, Libra, Aquarius

⋆ The Adult/Sun in **Gemini** is a versatile individual whose quick mind adapts to nearly everything. The sign of the twins, these individuals are often said to have dual sides and are quite changeable. They are well-informed, clever, and expressive, often with great communicative skills, but may spread themselves too thin. Well coordinated, they excel at the gentle sports such as golf and tennis as well as the parlor games of cards and backgammon, not to mention just plain playing games while talking. Restless, their attention can wander, drawing to them the criticism that they need more follow-through. However, this is the sign of the dexterous, the thinking, and the social.

⋆ Adult/Sun in **Libra** is the diplomat, the seeker of harmony. Sometimes criticized as indecisive, Libra is a perfectionist who likes consensus. They are very artistic and are most at home in social settings. They are cooperative and persuasive. Venus rules this sign and the romantic comes out in Libra, who loves love above all else. Accused of being a snob, the Libra will snip that it is merely a matter of good taste. The only sign of the Zodiac which is not a breathing creature, Librans have been accused of being cold and fickle, putting everything on the impersonal scales. Librans reply that good judgment must be impartial. Do not underestimate this sign—it is the master infighter and parlor wag.

⋆ Adult/Sun in **Aquarius** is imaginative and knowledgeable. These individuals are unpredictable, but so inventive that they appeal to the inner rebel in all of us. They can be very logical and progressive, with strong psychological tools of observation. They love to blow the horn for the downtrodden and abused. "Liberty and justice for all" is their motto. They can be excellent scientists and progressive parents. However, they are a fixed sign and once an Aquarian thinks the truth has been perceived, it is very difficult to change his or her mind, even with new facts, which are seen as an attempt to cloud the issue. These individuals need their space and are known for having love relationships which seem nontraditional compared to those of the rest of the Zodiac.

Child/Moon Ego Sphere

The Child/Moon ego sphere represents the Inner Child. The Moon/Child represents the emotional receiver in the chart, and by sign and aspect it will indicate how an individual goes about giving and receiving nurturing. The nature of an individual's emotional needs is reflected by the Inner Child/Moon. How trusting, how creative, how secure, how aggressive, how sensitive—these are the areas of the Inner Child.

Child/Moon ego in earth: Taurus, Virgo, Capricorn

⋆ Child/Moon in **Taurus** gives a emotional sense of the sensations of life, the pleasures, the tastes. Stubborn, but grounded in a resourceful and determined way, this Inner Child is charming and likes consistent, repetitive activities. Athletic and good-natured, they view change with suspicion. Honors old friendships and has lasting emotional bonds. Involvement with the material world is usually quite strong.

⋆ Child/Moon in **Virgo** is trustworthy, practical, analytical, and crafty. The reserve of emotional objectivity keeps the mind engaged in sifting the feelings for reasons and designs. There is a limiting control of the heat of emotional passion. Things are viewed from an analytical distance. Curiosity is actually a passion, and there is a need to know how things work. What is real and what is an illusion? This Inner Child wants to know more. The drive is for perfection (the virginal maiden) and can become a force of self-absorption. Romance is taken seriously and the gestures of love analyzed to such an extent as to sometimes hinder the spontaneity of the moment.

★ Child/Moon in **Capricorn** wants respect and can be quite reserved. Ambitious with the will to compete, the energy has discipline which is sometimes almost a shyness, but the need to succeed makes involvement necessary. A flair for control and a seriousness brings awkwardness to the expression of love. Gesture and emotion get confused. The gift is not only the expression of love but its measure.

Child/Moon ego in water: Cancer, Scorpio, Pisces

★ Child/Moon in **Cancer** is a sympathetic and sensitive individual who has powerful feelings that can sway with the tides. The emotion memory is very retentive and this Inner Child archetype can have difficulty letting go of old emotional material. The past can be too much for them. Great creativity and a strong sex drive makes for a person with dynamic magnetism. A brooding lover who wants it all, there can be a smothering quality if his or her attention is not modified by other factors. The intuition is strong and the religious fervor for spiritual release rivals that of ancient priestesses or priests of the mystery rites.

★ Child/Moon in **Scorpio** is powerful, charismatic, and potent. While often said to be the most sexual archetype, the real issue is not eros, but power. Sex is the power of the life force polarities connecting, male and female in union, the passing of the renewing and dying ember called life. Scorpio loves this, but it is the power to control many aspects of life, not just sex, that challenges it even more. This Inner Child wants to have it his or her own way. Money, reputation, influence, penetration—these are the motivations here. There is a strong ability to get to the bottom of things, to keep secrets, to be the agent of revealing and then solving a problem.

✴ Moon/Children in **Pisces** are very aware and imaginative. They feel more than they can articulate, creating a tension in expression. Often they turn to the arts for expression of their inner visions. Traditionally a psychic Child, the archetype is of mystic insights and revelations. Love can be painful because of the gap between feelings and their expression. Use of medicine, drugs, or even herbs can sometimes help relieve the tension, but can also lead to addiction or other forms of self-abuse, like alcoholism.

Child/Moon ego in fire: Aries, Leo, Sagittarius

✴ Moon/Child in **Aries** is an energetic and immediate archetype. Active and spontaneous, these are trailblazers who really self-start. However, this energy must be directed with self-control or the personality can tilt out of whack, subject to whim and appetite rather than planned direction. A potent lover with strong athletic skills, this type may worry that what runs so hot so fast can cool as easily, which is sometimes the case. Meditation is difficult, but active Eastern disciplines like the martial arts work out just fine.

✴ Moon/Child in **Leo** is a fixed sign with steady warmth and persevering energy that loves to shine, lead, and love. The self-concept is strong and a little vain, but the Zodiac needs a leader who is good-hearted, even if an egotist. While leadership is strong, so is the ability to entertain and amaze. Flash is Leo's middle name; this Inner Child loves attention. Creative and a lover of gifts, this person is a fun-loving romantic who has many social skills.

✴ Moon/Child in **Sagittarius** is a mutable sign which has an idealistic flair. The aim is high and the effort is pure. The heat of passion is strong, symbolized by the half-human, half-horse nature of the centaur. There is a directness of desire that can be disarming at first and endearing after a while. Focus is an issue as the fire energy here is seeking expression in many areas. Many talents can emerge: showperson, explorer, musician, lawyer, eccentric. This Inner Child is a loyal friend and a fearless ally when the chips are down. The ruler, Jupiter, expands this Moon into a constantly evolving matrix of mental and emotional surges toward personal truth.

Child/Moon ego in air: Gemini, Libra, Aquarius

★ Child/Moon in **Gemini** is a handful of energy, bubbling with curiosity. Versatile mental skills are motivated by an emotional need to know something about everything. Often witty and social, these Inner Children spread themselves thin. Accused of skating on the surface of issues, this individual is at best a sterling communicator; at worst, a gossip. Expression wins over feelings and breadth over depth. Good flirts, romance is their strong suit, but many relationships may be tried before one takes deep root in this mutable and emotional sign.

★ Child/Moon in **Libra** is affectionate, friendly, and romantic. This child will have a natural flair for artistic disciplines and is usually a very artistic dresser. A lover of harmony, it is hard to provoke this Child into an angry outburst. This Inner Child is a diplomat who will bring social pressure to bear on disputes. An excellent lover, the Child is a flirt who may be in love with love, as is its ruler, Venus. There is not the strong, decisive element here as much as there is a willingness to let everyone get their say and try to find a consensus.

★ Child/Moon in **Aquarius** is the inventive, emotionally structured individual. This Child is the psychologist, always seeking to understand others and their emotions. Emotions are difficult in this fixed air sign. Freedom and change are the battle cry for a surprisingly fixed emotional base. Ideas may be substituted for people to love. History, literature, whatever is loved is accepted highly and totally. Hugs are understood on a mental level, but not freely given. Love is the meeting of the minds in the mutual freedom to express themselves. Romance here resembles the anthropology of strange mental rituals. This Child loves best only if the heart and mind meet, for this Uranus-ruled archetype has mental attraction as a major part of its emotional make-up.

✫ ✭ ✫ **Appendix C** ☽ ☉ ◎ ♄

★ ✭ ☆ ✩ ☆ ★ ☆

Weighing the Aspects

★ ✭ ☆ ✩ ☆ ★ ☆

This section presents a dictionary of key words for the aspects, planets, and signs. The task of weighing the ego sphere has two steps. The first is to learn to weigh the ego sphere inner tension and mechanisms for release by defining the number and type of aspects made to each ego sphere. This will define the high focus sphere and the type of energy that is resident in it.

The second step is to learn to creatively link together key words into meaningful phrases which will provide insights into the nature of each of the aspects. The kaleidoscope of energies when captured in key words will reveal the scope and focus of the personality.

Types of Aspects

Hard: Conjunction, square, opposition

Dense: Inconjunction

Soft: Sextile, trine

Key Words

Hard:

Conjunction (0°): United, merged, melded, smoldering, intense, assimilated

Square (90°): Challenging, pressuring, contesting, clashing, encountering, motivating

Opposition (180°): Confronting, off-setting, conflicting, comparing, antagonizing, polarizing

Dense:

Inconjunction (150°): readjusting, diverging, interfering, rerouting, stressing, redirecting, stressing, disconcerting

Soft:

Sextile (60°): Helping, cooperating, stimulating, encouraging, opportunity, exciting

Trine (120°): Flowing, harmonizing, pooling, blending, interconnecting, compounding

Planets

Parent/Saturn:

Limits, security, rules, time, control, organization, responsibility

Adult/Sun:

Self-worth, assurance, vitality, spirit, leadership, identity

Child/Moon:

Receptive, instinctive, nurturing, emotions, compulsions, responsive

Mercury:

Communicates, gestures, thinks, questions, coordinates, perceives

Venus:

Indulges, charms, touches, harmonizes, possesses, senses, socializes

Mars:

Competes, pushes, lusts, impulses, asserts, initiates

Jupiter:

Expands, theorizes, explores, rewards, indulges, searches, directs

Uranus:

Freedom-loving, humanitarian, inventive, independent, willful, rebellious, stimulates

Neptune:

Idealistic, escapist, fantasy/illusion, visionary, magnetic, creative, sensitive, dependent

Pluto:

Transformation, charismatic, power, death/rebirth, depression, elation, projections, elimination, trauma, exploits, develops

Let's look at a couple of examples so that you can see that with these key words you can solve the puzzle of any chart.

Consider that you have Mercury square Parent/Saturn. Using the key words you would proceed with:

Square: Challenging, contesting

Mercury: Perceives, questions, communicates

Saturn: Authority, discipline

Now we put these together like this: Perceives, questions and challenges ways of communicating or contesting authority and discipline. See, the meaning just comes out at you!

The symbols for planets, aspects, and signs have become meaningful language about character traits. It looks simple, yet the results are very accurate. Learn this key word formula, add your own words to the list that you think are accurate for you, and you will see a world of meaning leap from each Tri-Astral analysis chart. It is an interpretive art which you can practice for years to come.

★ ★ ★ **Appendix D** ☽ ◉ ♄

★ ★ ☆ ☆ ☆ ☆ ★ ★

Symbols and Abbreviations

★ ★ ☆ ☆ ☆ ★ ★

Name............Abbreviation ......Symbol

Name............Abbreviation ......Symbol

Planets

Sun ....SU ....⊙

Moon ....MO ....☽

Mercury ....ME.................☿

Venus..............VE ....♀

Mars ....MA.................♂

Jupiter ....JU ....♃

Saturn ....SA.................♄

Uranus ....UR.................♅

Neptune ....NE ....♆

Pluto ....PL.................♇

Aspects

Conjunction .....Cj ....☌

Sextile.............Sx.................✳

Square.............Sq ....□

Trine................Tr ....△

Inconjunction ..Qx ....⊼
(Quincunx)

Opposition ......Op ....☍

Signs

Aries ....AR................♈

Taurus.............TA.................♉

Gemini ....GE ....♊

Cancer ....CN.................♋

Leo ....LE.................♌

Virgo ....VI ....♍

Libra ....LI ....♎

Scorpio............SC.................♏

Sagittarius.......SG ....♐

Capricorn ....CP ....♑

Aquarius ....AQ.................♒

Pisces...............PI.................♓

STAY IN TOUCH

On the following pages you will find listed, with their current prices, some of the books now available on related subjects. Your book dealer stocks most of these and will stock new titles in the Llewellyn series as they become available. We urge your patronage.

To obtain our full catalog, to keep informed about new titles as they are released and to benefit from informative articles and helpful news, you are invited to write for our bi-monthly news magazine/catalog, *Llewellyn's New Worlds of Mind and Spirit*. A sample copy is free, and it will continue coming to you at no cost as long as you are an active mail customer. Or you may subscribe for just $10.00 in U.S.A. and Canada ($20.00 overseas, first class mail). Many bookstores also have *New Worlds* available to their customers. Ask for it.

Llewellyn's New Worlds of Mind and Spirit
P.O. Box 64383-338, St. Paul, MN 55164-0383, U.S.A.

TO ORDER BOOKS AND TAPES

If your book dealer does not have the books described on the following pages readily available, you may order them direct from the publisher by sending full price in U.S. funds, plus $3.00 for postage and handling for orders under $10.00; $4.00 for orders over $10.00. There are no postage and handling charges for orders over $50.00. Postage and handling rates are subject to change. UPS Delivery: We ship UPS whenever possible. Delivery guaranteed. Provide your street address as UPS does not deliver to P.O. Boxes. UPS to Canada requires a $50.00 minimum order. Allow 4-6 weeks for delivery. Orders outside the U.S.A. and Canada: Airmail—add retail price of book; add $5.00 for each non-book item (tapes, etc.); add $1.00 per item for surface mail.

FOR GROUP STUDY AND PURCHASE

Because there is a great deal of interest in group discussion and study of the subject matter of this book, we feel that we should encourage the adoption and use of this particular book by such groups by offering a special quantity price to group leaders or agents.

Our special quantity price for a minimum order of five copies of *Astrology and the Games People Play* is $38.85 cash-with-order. This price includes postage and handling within the United States. Minnesota residents must add 6.5% sales tax. For additional quantities, please order in multiples of five. For Canadian and foreign orders, add postage and handling charges as above. Credit card (VISA, MasterCard, American Express) orders are accepted. Charge card orders only ($15.00 minimum order) may be phoned in free within the U.S.A. or Canada by dialing 1-800-THE-MOON. For customer service, call 1-612-291-1970. Mail orders to:

LLEWELLYN PUBLICATIONS
P.O. Box 64383-338, St. Paul, MN 55164-0383, U.S.A.

COMPUTERIZED ASTROLOGY REPORTS

Simple Natal APS03-119: Your chart calculated by computer in the Tropical/Placidus House system or the House system of your choice. It has all of the trimmings, including aspects, midpoints, Chiron and a glossary of symbols, plus a free booklet! $5.00

Personality Profile Horoscope APS03-503: Our most popular reading! This ten-part reading gives you a complete look at how the planets affect you. Learn about your general characteristics and life patterns. Look into your imagination and emotional needs. It is an excellent way to become acquainted with astrology and to learn about yourself. Very reasonable price! $20.00

Transit Forecasts: These reports keep you abreast of positive trends and challenging periods. Transit Forecasts can be an invaluable aid for timing your actions and decision making. Reports begin the first day of the month you specify.

3-month Transit Forecast APS03-500..............................$12.00
6-month Transit Forecast APS03-501..............................$20.00
1-year Transit Forecast APS03-502................................$25.00

Life Progressions APSO3-507: Discover what the future has in store for you! This incredible reading covers a year's time and is designed to complement the Personality Profile Reading. Progressions are a special system with which astrologers map how the "natal you" develops through specified periods of your present and future life, and with this report you can discover the "now you!" $20.00

Personal Relationship Reading APS03-506: If you've just called it quits on one relationship and know you need to understand more about yourself before you test the waters again, then this is the report for you! This reading will tell you how you approach relationships in general, what kind of people you look for and what kind of people might rub you the wrong way. Important for anyone! $20.00

Compatibility Profile APS03-504: Find out if you really are compatible with your lover, spouse, friend or business partner! This is a great way of getting an in-depth look at your relationship with another person. Find out each person's approach to the relationship. Do you have the same goals? How well do you deal with arguments? Do you have the same values? This service includes planetary placements for both individuals, so send birth data for both and specify the type of relationship (i.e., friends, lovers, etc.). Order today! $30.00

Numerology Report: Find out which numbers are right for you with this report. It uses an ancient form of numerology invented by Pythagoras to determine the significant numbers in your life. Using both your full birth name and date of birth, this report will accurately calculate those numbers which stand out as yours.

3-month Numerology Report APSO3-508 ....$12.00
6-month Numerology Report APSO3-509 ....$18.00
12-month Numerology Report APSO3-510 ....$25.00

Tarot Reading APS03-120: Find out what the cards have in store for you! This reading features the graphics of the traditional Rider-Waite card deck in a detailed 10-card spread, and as a bonus, there are three pages explaining what each Tarot card means for you. Specify a short question that you would like to have answered as well as the number of times you wish the deck to be shuffled. Order this exciting tarot reading today! **$10.00**

Lucky Lotto Report (State Lottery Report): Do you play the state lotteries? This report will determine your luckiest sequence of numbers for each day based on specific planets, degrees and other indicators in your own chart. Provide your full birth data and middle name, and specify the parameters of your state's lottery: i.e., how many numbers you need in sequence (up to 10 numbers) as well as the highest possible numeral (up to #999). Indicate the month you want to start.

3-month Lucky Lotto Report APS03-512..........................$10.00
6-month Lucky Lotto Report APS03-513..........................$15.00
12-month Lucky Lotto Report APS03-514.........................$25.00

Biorhythm Report: Ever have one of those days when you have unlimited energy and everything is going your way? Then the next day you are feeling sluggish and awkward? These cycles are called biorhythms. This individual report will accurately map your daily biorhythms. Each important day is thoroughly discussed. With this valuable information, you can schedule important events with great success. This report is an invaluable source of information to help you plan your days to the fullest. Order today!

3-month Biorhythm Report APS03-515 ....$12.00
6-month Biorhythm Report APS03-516 ....$18.00
12-month Biorhythm Report APS03-517 ....$25.00

Ultimate Astro-Profile APS03-505: This report has it all! Receive over 40 pages of fascinating, insightful and uncanny descriptions of your innermost qualities and talents. Read about your burn rate (thirst for change). Explore your personal patterns (inside and outside). Examine the particular pattern of your Houses. The Astro-Profile doesn't repeat what you've already learned from other personality profiles, but considers the often neglected natal influence of the lunar nodes, plus much more! **$40.00**

ASTROLOGICAL COUNSELING
The Path to Self-Actualization
Edited by Joan McEvers

This book explores the challenges for today's counselors and gives guidance to those interested in seeking an astrological counselor to help them win their own personal challenges. Includes articles by 10 well-known astrologers:

- **David Pond:** Astrological Counseling
- **Maritha Pottenger:** Potent, Personal Astrological Counseling
- **Bill Herbst:** Astrology and Psychotherapy: A Comparison for Astrologers
- **Gray Keen:** Plato Sat on a Rock
- **Ginger Chalford, Ph.D.:** Healing Wounded Spirits: An Astrological Counseling Guide to Releasing Life Issues
- **Donald L. Weston, Ph.D.:** Astrology and Therapy/Counseling
- **Susan Dearborn Jackson:** Reading the Body, Reading the Chart
- **Doris A. Hebel:** Business Counseling
- **Donna Cunningham:** The Adult Child Syndrome, Codependency, and Their Implications for Astrologers
- **Eileen Nauman:** Medical Astrology Counseling

0-87542-385-X, 304 pgs., 5¼ x 8, charts, softcover $14.95

THE ASTROLOGICAL THESAURUS, BOOK ONE
House Keywords
Michael Munkasey

Keywords are crucial for astrological work. They correctly translate astrological symbols into clear, everyday language—which is a never-ending pursuit of astrologers. For example, the Third House can be translated into the keywords "visitors," "early education," or "novelist."

The Astrological Thesaurus, Book One: House Keywords is a the first easy-to-use reference book and textbook on the houses, their psychologically rich meanings, and their keywords. This book also includes information on astrological quadrants and hemispheres, how to choose a house system, and the mathematical formulations for many described house systems.

Astrologer Michael Munkasey compiled almost 14,000 keywords from more than 600 sources over a 23-year period. He has organized them into 17 commonplace categories (e.g., things, occupations, and psychological qualities), and cross-referenced them three ways for ease of use: alphabetically, by house, and by category. Horary users, in particular, will find this book extremely useful.

0-87542-579-8, 434 pgs., 7 x 10, illus., softcover $19.95

EXPLORING CONSCIOUSNESS IN THE HOROSCOPE
edited by Noel Tyl

When Llewellyn asked astrologers across the country which themes to include in its "New World Astrology Series," most specified at the top of their lists themes that explore consciousness! From shallow pipedreaming to ecstatic transcendence, "consciousness" has come to envelop realms of emotion, imagination, dreams, mystical experiences, previous lives and lives to come—aspects of the mind which defy scientific explanation. For most, consciousness means self-realization, the "having it all together" to function individualistically, freely, and confidently.

There are many ways to pursue consciousness, to "get it all together." Astrology is an exciting tool for finding the meaning of life and our part within it, to bring our inner selves together with our external realities, in appreciation of the spirit. Here, then, ten fine thinkers in astrology come together to share reflections on the elusive quicksilver of consciousness. They embrace the spiritual—and the practical. All are aware that consciousness feeds our awareness of existence; that, while it defies scientific method, it is vital for life.

0-87542-391-4, 256 pgs., 6 x 9, tables, charts, softcover $12.00

HOW TO MANAGE THE ASTROLOGY OF CRISIS
edited by Noel Tyl

More often than not, a person will consult an astrologer during those times when life has become difficult, uncertain or distressing. While crisis of any type is really a turning point, not a disaster, the client's crisis of growth becomes the astrologer's challenge. By coming to the astrologer, the client has come to an oracle. At the very best, there is hope for a miracle; at the very least, there is hope for reinforcement through companionship and information. How do you as an astrological counselor balance a sober discussion of the realities with enthusiastic efforts to leave the client feeling empowered and optimistic?

In this, the eleventh title in Llewellyn's New World Astrology Series, eight renowned astrologers provide answers this question as it applies to a variety of life crises. *How to Manage the Astrology of Crisis* begins with a discussion of the birth-crisis, the first major transition crisis in everybody's life—their confrontation with the world. It then discusses significant family crises in childhood and healing of the inner child—mental crises including head injuries, psychological breakdown, psychic experiences, multiple personalities —career turning points and crises of life direction and action—astrological triggers of financial crisis and recent advances in financial astrology—astrological maxims for relationship crises—and the mid-life crises of creative space, idealism, and consciousness.

0-87542-390-6, 224 pgs., 6 x 9, charts, softcover $12.00

HOW TO PERSONALIZE THE OUTER PLANETS
The Astrology of Uranus, Neptune & Pluto
Edited by Noel Tyl

Since their discoveries, the three outer planets have been symbols of the modern era. Representing great social change on a global scale, they also take us as individuals to higher levels of consciousness and new possibilities of experience. Explored individually, each outer planet offers tremendous promise for growth. But when taken as a group, as they are in *Personalizing the Outer Planets*, the potential exists to recognize accelerated development.

As never done before, the seven prominent astrologers in *Personalizing the Outer Planets* bring these revolutionary forces down to earth in practical ways.

- **Jeff Jawer:** Learn how the discoveries of the outer planets rocked the world
- **Noel Tyl:** Project into the future with outer planet Solar Arcs
- **Jeff Green:** See how the outer planets are tied to personal trauma

- **Jeff Jawer:** Give perspective to your inner spirit through outer planet symbolisms
- **Jayj Jacobs:** Explore interpersonal relationships and sex through the outer planets
- **Mary E. Shea:** Make the right choices using outer planet transits
- **Joanne Wickenburg:** Realize your unconscious drives and urges through the outer planets
- **Capel N. McCutcheon:** Personalize the incredible archetypal significance of outer planet aspects

0-87542-389-2, 288 pgs., 6 x 9, illus., softcover...........................$12.00

THE HOUSES
Power Places of the Horoscope
Edited by Joan McEvers

The Houses are the departments of experience. The planets energize these areas—giving life meaning. Understand why you attract and are attracted to certain people by your 7th House cusp. Go back in time to your 4th House, the history of your beginning. Joan McEvers has ingeniously arranged the chapters to show the Houses' relationships to each other and the whole. Various house systems are briefly described in Joan McEvers' introduction. Learn about house associations and planetary influences upon each house's activities with the following experts.

- **Peter Damian:** The First House and the Rising Sun
- **Ken Negus:** The Seventh House
- **Noel Tyl:** The Second House and The Eighth House
- **Spencer Grendahl:** The Third House
- **Dona Shaw:** The Ninth House
- **Gloria Star:** The Fourth House
- **Marwayne Leipzig:** The Tenth House
- **Lina Accurso:** Exploring Your Fifth House
- **Sara Corbin Looms:** The Eleventh: House of Tomorrow
- **Michael Munkasey:** The Sixth House
- **Joan McEvers:** The Twelfth House: Strength, Peace, Tranquillity

0-87542-383-3, 400 pgs., 5¼ x 8, illus., softcover........................$12.95

MYTHIC ASTROLOGY
Archetypal Powers in the Horoscope
Ariel Guttman & Kenneth Johnson

Here is an entirely new dimension of self-discovery based on understanding the mythic archetypes represented in the astrological birth chart. Myth has always been closely linked with astrology; all our planets are named for the Graeco-Roman deities and derive their interpretative meanings from them. To richly experience the myths which lie at the heart of astrology is to gain a deeper and more spiritual perspective on the art of astrology and on life itself.

Mythic Astrology is unique because it allows the reader to explore the connection between astrology and the spirituality of myth in depth, without the necessity of a background in astrology, anthropology or the classics. This book is an important contribution to the continuing study of mythology as a form of New Age spirituality and is also a reference work of enduring value. Students of mythology, the Goddess, art, history, Jungian psychological symbolism and literature—as well as lovers of astrology—will all enjoy the text and numerous illustrations.

0-87542-248-9, 382 pgs., 7 x 10, 100 illus., softcover......................$17.95

PLANETS
The Astrological Tools
Edited by Joan McEvers

This is the second in the astrological anthology series edited by respected astrologer Joan McEvers, who provides a brief factual overview of the planets. Then take off through the solar system with 10 professional astrologers as they bring their insights to the symbolism and influences of the planets.

- **Toni Glover Sedgwick:** The Sun as the life force and our ego
- **Joanne Wickenburg:** The Moon as our emotional signal to change
- **Erin Sullivan-Seale:** Mercury as the multifaceted god, followed with an in-depth explanation of its retrogradation
- **Robert Glasscock:** Venus as your inner value system and relationships
- **Johanna Mitchell:** Mars as your cooperative, energizing inner warrior
- **Don Borkowski:** Jupiter as expansion and preservation
- **Gina Ceaglio:** Saturn as a source of freedom through self-discipline
- **Bil Tierney:** Uranus as the original, growth-producing planet
- **Karma Welch:** Neptune as selfless giving and compassionate love
- **Joan Negus:** Pluto as a powerful personal force

0-87542-381-7, 384 pgs., 5¼ x 8, softcover $12.95

SPIRITUAL, METAPHYSICAL & NEW TRENDS IN MODERN ASTROLOGY
Edited by Joan McEvers

This is the first book in Llewellyn's New World Astrology Series. Edited by well-known astrologer, lecturer and writer Joan McEvers, this book pulls together the latest thoughts by the best astrologers in the field of Spiritual Astrology.

- **Gray Keen:** Perspective: The Ethereal Conclusion
- **Marion D. March:** Some Insights Into Esoteric Astrology
- **Kimberly McSherry:** The Feminine Element of Astrology: Reframing the Darkness
- **Kathleen Burt:** The Spiritual Rulers and Their Role in the Transformation
- **Shirley Lyons Meier:** The Secrets Behind Carl Payne Tobey's Secondary Chart
- **Jeff Jawer:** Astrodrama
- **Donna Van Toen:** Alice Bailey Revisited
- **Philip Sedgwick:** Galactic Studies
- **Myrna Lofthus:** The Spiritual Programming Within a Natal Chart
- **Angel Thompson:** Transformational Astrology

0-87542-380-9, 264 pgs., 5¼ x 8, softcover $9.95

WEB OF RELATIONSHIPS
Spiritual, Karmic & Psychological Bonds
edited by Joan McEvers

The astrology of intimacy has long been a popular subject among professional astrologers and psychologists. Many have sought the answer to what makes some people have successful relationships with one another, while others struggle. *Web of Relationships* examines this topic not only in intimate affiliations, but also in families and friendships, in this eighth volume of the Llewellyn New World Astrology Series.

Editor Joan McEvers has brought together the wisdom and experience of eight astrology experts. Listen to what one author says about the mythological background of planets as they pertain to relationships. Discover how past life regression is illustrated in the chart. Consider the relationship of astrology and transactional analysis.

Web of Relationships explores the karmic and mystical connections between child and parent, how friends support and understand each other, the significance of the horoscope as it pertains to connections and much more. Each chapter will bring you closer to your own web of relationships and the astrology of intimacy.

0-87542-388-4, 240 pgs., 6 x 9, softcover...................................**$14.95**

YOUR PLANETARY PERSONALITY
Everything You Need to Make Sense of Your Horoscope
by Dennis Oakland

This book deepens the study of astrological interpretation for professional and beginning astrologers alike. Dennis Oakland's interpretations of the planets in the houses and signs are the result of years of study of psychology, sciences, symbolism, Eastern philosophy plus the study of birth charts from a psychotherapy group. Unlike the interpretations in other books, these emphasize the life processes involved and facilitate a greater understanding of the chart. Includes 100-year ephemeris.

Even if you now know *nothing* about astrology, Dennis Oakland's clear instructions will teach you how to construct a complete and accurate birth chart for anyone born between 1900 to 1999. After you have built your chart, he will lead you through the steps of reading it, giving you indepth interpretations of each of your planets. When done, you will have the satisfaction that comes from increased self-awareness and from being your *own* astrologer!

This book is also an excellent exploration for psychologists and psychiatrists who use astrology in their practices.

0-87542-594-1, 580 pgs., 7 x 10, softcover...............................**$19.95**